THE BAD INVESTMENT GUIDE

OR HOW *not* TO INVEST YOUR MONEY

TED LAKE, ACIS, ACIB, ASFA

OLD BAILEY PRESS

OLD BAILEY PRESS LIMITED
200 Greyhound Road, London, W14 9RY

First published 2000

© Ted Lake 2000

ISBN 1 85836 359 4

British Library Cataloguing-in-Publication.

A CIP Catalogue record for this book is available from the British
Library.

Printed and bound in Great Britain.

Contents

By the Same Author   *v*

Preface   *vii*

Acknowledgments   *ix*

1 The Aims and Purpose of This Book   *1*

2 Some Rules of Investment and Definitions   *4*

3 The Damaging Effects of Inflation   *7*

4 The Dangers of Fixed Rates and Tying Money Up   *11*

5 Some Drawbacks to ISAs, National Savings and PEP Transfers   *15*

6 Are Investment Risks Worth It?   *21*

7 The Need to Monitor Investments   *31*

8 Living with Investment Risk   *38*

9 Unit Trusts and OEICs   *41*

10 Single Premium Policies or Bonds and Life Assurance Funds   *56*

11 Investment Trusts   *62*

12 Higher-Risk Investment Schemes   *74*

13 High-Income Bonds and Higher-Income Bonds   *80*

14 Direct Investments in Stocks and Shares (Equities)   *82*

15 Investing in Gilts   *92*

16 Guaranteed Investment Products   *100*

17 Ethical Investments   *105*

18 Investing in Property   *109*

19 Investing Offshore   *120*

20 Investments Held in a Trust   *128*

21 Investing for Children   *132*

22 Income Tax and Capital Gains Tax Planning   *136*

23 Do It Yourself or Take Investment Advice?   *149*

24 Have I Got the Strategy Right?   *156*

Appendices

1 UK Financial History 1945–1998   *165*

2 Record of Past Growth in the UK Stock Market as Demonstrated by Some Collective Investment Schemes   *167*

3 Indexation Table for Capital Gains Tax   *176*

4 Record of Annual Inflation and the Retail Price Index (RPI)   *178*

5 Guide to National Savings   *180*

6 Details of Some Zero Dividend Preference Shares (ZDPs)   *182*

7 Staircase of Investment Risk   *184*

8 Risk Warning Notice   *185*

9 The Costs of Buying and Selling Shares   *187*

10 An Explanation of the Price/Earnings Ratio (P/E Ratio)   *191*

11 A Brief Explanation of Derivatives   *193*

Index   *195*

By the Same Author

An Introduction to Financial Services

The Giving of Financial Advice

Written for 'independent' and 'tied' advisers and those for have just started or are considering a career in the financial services industry. The book is also aimed at those students on degree or HND courses in banking or business studies and which have a financial services content. It will be of interest to lecturers and writers on financial matters.

Preface

The aims and purpose of this book are set out in Chapter 1. However, it should be made clear that in writing this book I have assumed some financial knowledge on the part of readers. The degree of such knowledge will vary, but to include an explanation or a definition for every financial term used would have made the text too long and would, I feel, detract from the message conveyed within. Although I have explained about new unit trust sectors in detail, I have not felt it appropriate to define (for instance) the 'RPI' or FSAVCs. Standard investment and financial abbreviations have been used throughout and I trust that most readers will be familiar with those.

This book is a serious attempt to stimulate readers to take a closer interest in precisely how, where and why their funds are invested. The enormous differences between investment returns cannot be stressed enough. Obtaining an additional (for example) 5 per cent per annum by means of a better investment policy or better tax planning can build up to a large sum over many years.

Whilst every effort has been made to ensure accuracy and provide an up-to-date text, the author and publisher cannot accept any liability for errors or omissions or changes in detail or from any consequences arising from the use of the information contained herein.

It is of course inevitable that future legislation and taxation changes will have a bearing on both the detail and the various points made. Nevertheless the text has been written, so far as is possible, to stress the general nature of the advice and suggestions offered and I hope that readers will be able to adapt the message to future changes.

The writer would welcome comments or suggestions that might be of use in a future edition.

Ted Lake, ACIS, ACIB, ASFA

January 2000

Acknowledgements

The author would like to acknowledge the help, advice and encouragement received from the following in the preparation of this book.

My friends, MJ McChrystal, ACIB; Ron G Gates, ACIB; Roger J Munnerley, ACII; and John Dean, BA, MSc, for their help and encouragement.

Micropal, for kind permission to use their statictics. Schroder Unit Trusts, Perpetual Unit Trusts Ltd, M & G Group Ltd, Sun Life Assurance Ltd, Barclays Capital, CMI Insurance Co Ltd, Scottish Widows Group Ltd.

Anne McMeeham, The Association of Unit Trusts and Investment Funds.

Annabel Brodie-Smith, The Association of Investment Trust Companies.

Karen Eldridge, Ethical Investment Research Service.

Paul Keeble, Press Officer at the Department of National Savings.

David Parker, Senior Partner, Rawsthorns Solicitors, Preston.

Tim Scott, MSI, Dip, Hedley & Co Stockbrokers, Preston.

Michael J Drakeford, ACIB, Head of Compliance at a major UK Bank.

Richard Garside FRICS, IRRV; Kevin Eastham, ARIBA, FRTPI; and Peter Bramworth CEng, MSc, all of whom contributed to the chapter on investing in property.

My wife Wendy for long absences spent on writing.

1 Aims and Purpose of This Book

Some people think of themselves as 'investors' some as 'savers' but many in the latter category will be holders of some ordinary shares (equities) acquired during the privatisation programme of the 1980s and the 1990s. Some will hold shares in the company they work for, acquired through SAYE schemes, employees' share schemes and some will have inherited shares. Throughout this book I have made no attempt to distinguish between the two!

Even those who do not, and do not wish to hold any ordinary shares, unit trusts or other risk-based investments may still, from time to time, consider moving their savings into TESSAs, ISAs, National Savings accounts etc.

Anyone who reads the newspapers cannot fail to notice all the advertisements and articles extolling individual bank and building society accounts together with their PEPs TESSAs, ISAs, high-income bonds and so on. The weekend press has pages and supplements devoted to personal finance. All readers will have received mailings and television has never had so many programmes on money matters.

In short, everyone wants your money, and many claim to have the best products. Financial journalists write pages about the merits of with-profit bonds but no one tells you what NOT to invest in. Nor indeed, having made any 'investment' (in the widest sense of that word) why, when and how you should check up on its progress and performance.

It is fully accepted that under the UK's current regulatory system no investment advice should be offered by any adviser unless both qualified and authorised under the provisions of the Financial Services Act (FSA) 1986. No such advice should be offered without a full investigation into a person's circumstances which should establish:

1. general financial situation, jobs, incomes, dependents etc;
2. a person's attitude to risk;
3. investor's aims and objectives;
4. time horizons;

5. income tax position;
6. all or any existing investments, savings and pension provisions.

Nevertheless, all bank and building society savings schemes plus TESSAs, National Savings products and now some ISAs do not fall within the scope of the FSA 1986 and do not require advice. Also, some people invest on an execution-only basis.

In recent years we have seen the issue of 'Best PEP guides', 'Best TESSA guides' and 'Best with-profit bond guides'. Usually such guides are careful not to actually give out any advice but merely provide financial data on charges and past performance and then let the readers decide for themselves. Some offer generous commission-sharing terms. While I do not wish to disparage any of these guides, indeed the data they present is often very useful and an aid to good investment, they simply cannot include any 'weightings' relating to someone's personal circumstances. In addition there must be some chance that the apparent commission share will persuade investors into less than the best course of action.

So, although many want your money and many more are ready to suggest how you should invest your money, hardly anyone tells you what NOT to invest in! That is the purpose of this book.

Having spent a working life in finance, mostly in banking, latterly as a bank manager followed by eight years as an Independent Financial Adviser (IFA) with a large firm of solicitors, coupled with an active interest in the Stock Exchange for many years, I do feel able to write on this topic and do so based upon many years of experience.

Over all that time, I continued to be surprised at the number of poor investment decisions which people make with the consequent financial loss, or, if no actual loss, in foregoing the far better returns available elsewhere. This is linked to the more understandable failure to monitor the progress of investments and to take sensible action when needed. Such action could include:

1. realising gains when possible and utilising the annual capital gains tax exemption;
2. selling/reducing overly large holdings to reduce investment risk;
3. failing to use the various 'tax breaks' available from time to time;
4. leaving overly large sums on 'instant access' when much less would suffice;
5. leaving large sums in low-earning accounts;

6. non-taxpayers investing in National Savings Certificates and, arguably, TESSAs;
7. leaving all, or nearly all, capital in deposit-based accounts for many years, to be eroded by inflation coupled with no protection against falling interest rates;
8. failing to change investments to meet changing circumstances.

This list is not exhaustive, nor is the list in any sort of priority, but it at least serves to illustrate how investments are easily mismanaged. The areas included will all be covered in later chapters.

This book does not set out to tell readers how to invest their money but instead to offer practical help in overall financial planning and to avoid the mistakes that I have seen so many customers, clients, friends and myself make over the years.

There is really no doubt at all that the difference resulting from good investment decisions and poor ones can be very large indeed. I recognise that luck as well as good judgement will always play a part. Nevertheless the results of some poor or just plain silly investment decisions have been breathtaking to say the least!

Occasionally, reference is made to the past performance of some particular share, unit trust or life fund which is included in order to provide an example or to illustrate a point and implies no suggestion whatsoever that a reader should rush into making an investment in that product. When considering any stock exchange-linked, risk-based investment it should be clearly understood that past performance is not necessarily a guide to future investment performance. The price of shares and of units and the income from them can go down as well as up as a result of changes in the value of underlying securities or currencies and it is possible that investors may not get back the amount originally invested.

The Bad Investment Guide or How NOT to Invest Your Money is about lump-sum investments of all types and so no effort has been made to include advice or comments on pension planning or mortgages. Those are quite separate matters.

Pension planning is complex due to the number of schemes available coupled with the current Government proposals on 'stakeholder pensions' and uncertainty about the future of SERPS and the Second State Pension. Until those matters are clarified, it is difficult to offer any comments on pension planning except to emphasise the overriding need for all of us to have adequate pension provisions in place. The only further reference to pensions in the text is in the general area of tax planning.

2 Some Rules of Investment and Definitions

Most people would agree that investment is not an exact science, if indeed a science at all. There is room for differing opinions on the relative merits, risks and rewards of differing investments and all advisers and existing or likely investors will be entitled to apply their own measures and yardsticks.

Nevertheless, it is suggested that there are a few 'rules' or principles which seem to be very sound and have stood the test of time. All investors would do well to bear the following in mind when assessing an existing investment, considering a new one or switching an investment.

Rules of investment

RULE 1   **Nothing goes up for ever.** With risk-based investments, shares, unit trusts etc, what goes up comes down eventually. The quicker prices rise the more likely and quicker they are to fall.

RULE 2   **Don't have all your investment eggs in one basket.** The risk of all or most investments in one basket is clear – so spread the risk. This rule can apply to totally risk-free investors who will only consider deposit-based investments.

RULE 3   **Be aware that inflation is still a major investment risk.** Steps should be taken to reduce this danger to one's funds. The longer the time horizons, the greater the danger of inflation.

RULE 4   **Review investments regularly.** Monitor the performance of your investments regularly and take positive steps to deal with changing circumstances.

RULE 5   **Take profits and minimise losses.**

RULE 6   **Never invest solely to save tax.** Instead look for sound and suitable investments and then try to arrange them in a tax-efficient way.

Some of my 'rules' overlap, some are included because often investors just cannot be bothered or are too busy to attend to their affairs. For some, there is a real lack of interest or an inability to get to grips with the matter. Writing as someone who has been interested in investment for many years, I believe that nearly all investors are guilty of ignoring at least some of my rules and many ignore them all.

Of course if you break any of these rules you will not get fined, cautioned or punished in any way. Indeed many will be quite happy to leave such matters totally untouched for years at a time and only take some action when forced to do so. What I do suggest very strongly, and which is the purpose of this book, is to try to encourage readers to be more positive about their investments and not to fall into the traps of neglect discussed later.

Definitions used in this book

Deposit-based investments
(often referred to as 'savings')

Bank, building society accounts, TESSAs, National Savings products. Capital values never fluctuate and there is no 'investment risk'. The investment/deposit account is always the original sum lodged plus interest or possibly some other 'bonus'.

Asset-backed investments

Direct investment into individual stocks and shares plus other stock exchange listed investments including units in unit trusts, units in life funds and higher-income bonds where return of capital is linked to one or more stock exchange index. Includes money purchase pension plans and FSAVCs.

Best advice

Although the words 'best advice' have been used throughout this book and are in general use within the financial services industry, no precise definition exists. However the meaning is clear.

There is now a trend for the less emotive terms of 'suitable advice' or 'good advice' to be used instead.

An investor

There is no precise definition in law or in the Financial Services Act. It seems to apply to a person who has or is acquiring some capital which is to be placed in a deposit-backed investment or an asset-backed investment and not spent immediately. The motivation could be a general desire to save or linked to a particular objective or time-span.

Financial Services Act 1986

The principal Act of Parliament (referred to throughout this book as the 'FSA') which controls the working of the financial services industry in the UK. It is shortly to be superseded by a new Financial Services and Markets Act.

Collective investment schemes

This is a generic term applied when funds placed in asset-backed invest-ments are done so through some sort of scheme which 'pools' the funds from numerous individual investors and then manages them in accordance with a pre-determined investment policy. Such schemes are unit trusts, OEICs, life insurance funds, distribution bonds and with-profit bonds.

Investment trusts have some of the characteristics of a collective invest-ment scheme plus some of the features of direct investment into stocks and shares.

3 The Damaging Effects of Inflation

Readers who can recall the 1970s, particularly if they were in work, will remember the dreadful days when the UK's inflation rate reached almost 27% pa. The writer well remembers shopping in supermarkets and seeing goods on the shelves with four price tags, one on top of the other, each increasing the price.

For those in certain employment sectors times were not so hard, since many like myself received large cost of living rises as well as annual incremental rises or had pay rises linked to promotion. So, when the stock market did well and property prices soared as in the early 1970s and for much of the 1980s, the 'feel-good' factor was born.

Of course it wasn't good for everybody. Those in work where pay rises were small lost out, pensioners and others on fixed incomes saw a real decline in their standard of living as their fixed income bought less and less. Those whose pensions were fully index-linked (mainly civil servants, teachers and local government officers etc) suddenly realised the incredible benefit of an index-linked pension.

It is outside the scope of this book to investigate the root causes of inflation and the various fiscal and monetary devices available to try to control and hopefully eliminate it. In those days of high inflation, to leave large sums invested in building societies or other fixed interest investments was inviting financial disaster.

However, at the time of writing, inflation has been successfully reduced to a very low level of around 3% both in the UK and throughout most of the developed world. As a result, inflation is scarcely relevant for investors in the short term BUT in the medium to longer term it does remain a problem. The larger the funds invested or to be invested and the longer the time span, the greater the significance.

Apart from weighing up the possible effects of inflation, investment decisions are heavily influenced by time horizons. Those saving/investing for a known purpose – for example an expensive holiday, a new car or marriage – will have little need to worry about inflation at the present time.

For others, whose time horizons exceed five years, the effects of inflation should be borne in mind. Over much longer periods of 15–20 years the implications are undoubtedly serious as the following 'Effects of inflation' table makes clear.

Effects of inflation

The following table shows what £1,000 will be worth in today's money at the end of the period shown, if the annual rate of inflation over the period is as indicated:

Period in Years	Rate of Inflation		
	4%	7%	10%
	£	£	£
5	822	713	621
10	676	508	386
15	555	362	239
20	456	258	149
25	375	184	92
30	308	131	57
35	253	94	36
40	208	67	22
45	171	48	14
50	141	34	9

Anyone retiring in their 50s with a time horizon/life expectancy of 20–30 years will see the value of their funds wrecked if all are in deposit-based savings accounts. This would have serious implications for one's heirs! The problem is not of course confined to those retiring early. Anyone receiving a legacy in their 30s or 40s may well decide to spend some immediately and some later, but an amount may be invested long term, perhaps to boost income in retirement in up to 30 years' time. A glance at the table above shows that even if inflation were never to exceed 4% pa, then over the long term money loses most of its value.

The same problem exists when young children inherit money, which of course they cannot actually receive until they reach to the age of 18 at the earliest. Very often testators stipulate a later age of 21 or 25, in which case the trustees will have to invest prudently for up to 25 years.

If no income is to be paid out, then index-linked gilts may be appropriate for some of the funds, but many sensible trustees would wish to invest some of the trust funds, aiming for capital growth to exceed inflation if the amount and timespans are both appropriate.

I have dwelt at length upon the adverse effect of inflation because the very existence of this problem is the main reason for taking investment risks with one's money. Having read a number of books offering investment advice and guidance, this topic is rarely adequately explained and covered, nor are the long-term effects spelt out.

The problem is not a new one. As any student of history knows inflation was a problem in the reign of Queen Elizabeth I. Although now well under control, many involved in financial matters believe that it will re-occur eventually. A further problem is that whatever the rate of inflation, you can never actually see it, but it is there all the time nibbling away at one's funds! Few of us have the time or inclination to monitor the position regularly and then take a decision to move the money invested and so the problem is left to get worse.

A table of the past levels of inflation (the RPI) since 1985 is included in the appendices (Appendix 4) and readers who have had significant sums lodged in deposit-based accounts for many years could take a few moments to calculate and assess the effects of inflation upon their funds. Please be warned that this is apt to be a rather depressing exercise and may well cause some readers to re-assess their investment strategies, which is one aim of this book.

An illustration of the effects of inflation on an investment of £20,000 between June 1989 and June 1999

RPI June 1989	115.4
RPI June 1999	165.6
Increase	50.2 = 43%
Original capital	£20,000
Effect of inflation – reduction of 43%	£ 8,600
Purchasing power of £20,000 is now	£11,400

In simple terms the £20,000 has lost nearly half of its value and that reduced value continues to fall all the time. The effect of inflation on income is as bad or worse. The purchasing power of the annual income:

1. varies with interest rates;
2. enjoys no tax advantages;
3. suffers the same degree of loss.

In 1988 the average interest rate was around 10% pa so the initial income on a £20,000 investment was £2,000 pa.

By 1999 the average income was reduced to about 6% = £1,200 pa.

That was then reduced by inflation by about 43% to £680 pa.

So the original £20,000 capital plus the initial income of £2,000 pa have shrunk to £11,400 plus £684 in just ten years!

Various charts and graphs in the appendices set out the effects of inflation over longer periods. At this point readers may wish to compare these gloomy figures with the results which have been obtained from asset-backed investments over the same ten-year period. For comparative purposes figures are included from Schroders, Perpetual, M & G and Sun Life together with the growth in the various sectors for all unit trusts, investment trusts and the stock market generally as shown in the growth of the FTSE 100 index. Note that the figures for Schroders are given on page 23.

4 The Dangers of Fixed Rates and Tying Money Up

Overview

Most investors try to invest wisely and some are attracted to various fixed-rate offers available from time to time which seem attractive. There are of course two very obvious snags:

1. interest rates generally can move upwards, making the fixed-rate deal no longer attractive, and better alternatives become available;

2. even if the above does not occur the investor may need the funds for whatever reason and may be unable to access them, or obtain access subject to penalties which may be so heavy as to totally negate the previously expected benefits.

Those who design and promote fixed-rate products usually set the penalties at a sufficiently high level so as to act as a real deterrent. Otherwise many would simply suffer a small penalty for the benefit of breaking the savings scheme contract.

Fixed rates/stepped rates

Fixed rates and stepped rates usually look attractive when first offered. That is because they are structured and marketed to appear attractive but care is needed. Investors should compare the fixed rate or the average stepped rate with the 'going rate' which will probably be the best '90 days notice' account and then decide carefully if the excess offered justifies tying the funds up. Whether or not the fixed/stepped rate is attractive must be a matter of opinion, but I always think that a good 'premium' is needed to justify the downside risks. A study of the past trend in interest rates shows only too clearly how quickly interest rates can rise – they never seem to fall as quickly!

A further point, when considering these schemes, is to bear in mind the current level of interest rates compared with the historical norm. This is not an exact matter but the point to make here is that when interest rates are historically very high they are much more likely to fall than to rise further and vice versa. So to tie funds up in either of these schemes, when rates are historically low, seems much less sensible as when rates are historically high.

Product providers want these products to make money for them, not to lose them money, so they will always be careful to market both schemes at times most favourable to them, ie when they believe that interest rates are likely to rise within the life span of the product. The questions investors should ask themselves are these: by how much must other interest rates rise before this product has lost its attraction to me and is that likely to occur?

The answer will always be a matter of opinion, but it does seem to be unwise to tie funds up for (say) five years to gain a small added incentive of 1%–2% if a similar rise would wipe out all the benefits.

An historical example puts the matter in perspective. In 1991 our interest rates were sky high. Building societies were paying a massive 14% on some accounts and up to 15% on TESSAs. Clearly, interest rates would probably fall and probably fall significantly. Guaranteed income bonds were paying 11% pa net for five years with virtually no investment risk. As an Independent Financial Adviser, I moved some clients' funds into such fixed-rate products. Interest rates then fell steadily until banks/building societies were paying 6% gross. Those clients in the guaranteed income bonds were very satisfied clients indeed. This is not to claim financial brilliance but merely to apply some financial common sense. The principle works well with gilts. When interest rates are high, the price of gilts is depressed and when interest rates fall the price of gilts increase so that now gilts are all at an unbelievabe 30-year high. As they are fixed-interest investments the income stream will not have changed, but some investors are sitting on a very nice capital gain free from CGT!

Stepped interest accounts

These schemes have been around in various forms for some years. They generally offer an initial return less than the 'going-rate' which then increases each year, but the capital is tied up for four or five years. The marketing ploy is to emphasise the final top rate, which is paid out for only one year, but could be less, perhaps nine months. They may, in very small print, show the overall average return, but they may not! That is of course the figure which must be considered when using the tests set out above. These are not an inherently bad investment provided that the average return is attractive, but often it is not that much better than is available in a less restrictive account.

At the time of writing one leading UK bank is offering, for £10,000, an escalator bond as follows:

1st year	£4.05 %
2nd year	£4.15 %
3rd year	£4.90 %
4th year	£7.05 %
5th year	£9.50 %

Of course the brochure stresses the 9.5% but the average is 5.93% and at that time some lenders were offering 7.5% on instant access. Of course the instant access rate can and probably will fall – BUT it has to fall by a massive 2.5% before that escalator bond shows any benefit and in the meantime the funds are tied up for five years. So while it may appeal to some, it looks unattractive to me and deserves this mention in the *Bad Investment Guide*.

The dangers of tying all of one's money up

As an IFA, I ran various investment seminars for clients of the solicitors' practice and also talked to new clients regularly. The firm sent newsletters to clients which contained investment suggestions. On numerous occasions clients said to me that that were very interested in some particular investment opportunity but all of their funds were tied up in order to maximise their returns.

Whether or not the additional interest earned was significant was rarely clear, but what is very clear indeed is that the investment scene changes all the time. This applies not just to interest rates but to inflation levels and any tax breaks and new products available. As a result it seems that to tie up all (or most) of one's funds for a long time must of necessity reduce room to manoeuvre in order to take advantage of any of these changes, including new products.

There are those, however, who are always attracted to the extra income to be earned from tying funds up and also from lodging funds in larger individual deposits as most schemes pay tiered rates, ie more for larger deposits above certain thresholds.

There is no clear solution to this except to consider not tying up money in one or two large investments but instead aiming for smaller investments with a pattern of regular maturities, for example every year or every other year. That will go some way to improving liquidity and the opportunity to take advantage of the ever-changing investment scene.

5 Some Drawbacks to ISAs, National Savings and PEP Transfers

Investment Savings Accounts (ISAs)

ISAs were launched in April 1999 when PEPs and TESSAs were withdrawn. ISAs offer a small 'saving' on income tax probably for five years, plus a possible saving on capital gains tax indefinitely. The income tax saved will be the 10% tax credit currently attached to the dividends on ordinary shares. That 10% tax credit will satisfy the income tax liability at 20% (for savings income) and 23% for earned income, but will meet the added liability to higher rate tax for those on the top tax rate of 40%, who will have an additional 32.5% tax liability.

Although ISAs were politically motivated to spread the savings habit, particularly amongst those who traditionally had little or no savings, the outcome seems likely to have the reverse effect and make ISAs most attractive to higher-rate taxpayers!

For savings-rate and earnings-rate taxpayers, the income tax saved is really very modest. The ISA limit in the first year (1999/2000) is £7,000, thereafter £5,000. Looking at the ceiling of £5,000 the saving is easily worked out:

£5,000 at 3.0% * = £150 pa @ 10% (tax saved) is £15 pa.

*The rate of 3.0% is the average return on all UK Equity Income unit trusts as at August 1999 taken from Micropal's statistics in *Money Management*.

The savings are scarcely worthwhile in order to save income tax. The CGT position may well be different. While there is an annual exemption of (currently) £7,100, an investment of £5,000 in an ISA has to do extraordinarily well for the CGT exemption to be of any benefit. However, for someone with significant CGT liabilities and who is considering making an investment, to be able to wrap it up in an ISA could be a significant advantage, but that seems to be the only real benefit. Of course, readers will have to make up their own minds, but I consider that ISAs justify a mention in this book.

Corporate bond funds in an ISA

This seems to be the best option for saving income tax using an ISA. The benefits are as follows:

£5,000 @ 5.8% # = £290 @ 20% * = £58 pa tax saved.

Average return on UK General Bonds unit trust sector as at August 1999.

* Present savings tax rate.

However, the point to bear in mind here is the almost a certain lack of both income growth and capital growth, and the maximum sum which can be invested this way at £5,000 pa will be inconveniently low for many investors.

Placing life insurance products in an ISA

The general consensus is that this option has little or no merit. The amount is just too small to have much appeal to most investors. However, insurance companies are bound to keep that marketing opportunity under review. At the time of writing they are lobbying the Government to increase the permitted maximum of £1,000 pa and so this investment opportunity may change.

National Savings

National Savings (a Government Department) has been with us for many years and offers a wide range of investment/savings schemes designed to appeal to:

- Non-taxpayers
- Basic rate taxpayers
- Higher rate taxpayers
- Pensioners

Various products offer:

- A regular monthly income
- Income paid out less often
- Income rolled-up
- Index linking
- Tax-free returns

From time to time some products are very attractive and others less so, and at other times some qualify for the investment equivalent of a wooden spoon! The general level of return will be influenced by the Government's need to borrow money. If the need is not great (in boom/growth conditions) then the overall returns will be less generous, although there is a need to remain competitive to achieve sales in order to meet maturities and repayments.

However, all National Savings products need to be examined carefully to assess their real attractions in order to make comparisons with other investment opportunities. At the time of writing, none seem to be attractive except possibly Premium Savings Bonds (for gamblers!) and National Savings Income Bonds which offer 5.05% gross but are taxable and paid monthly.

The launch of Pensioners Guaranteed Income Bonds saw a leading politician say that such bonds aimed to give the pensioners 'a decent rate of return'. Now that 'decent' rate of return is just 5.65% pa and fixed for five years!!!

For some cautious investors National Savings products may be the answer but all readers will be advised to look elsewhere when funds are to be invested.

At the time of writing, the press is full of articles on ISAs. The Government clearly wants this new savings vehicle to mirror the success of PEPs, and in particular they want to see the success of CAT-marked ISAs. CAT marking stands for 'charges, access and terms' all of which must meet Government standards aimed at being fair to investors.

Ironically none of the existing range of National Savings products could be put into an ISA because none meet the CAT marking standards! Maybe that does not matter to many individual investors but it amply demonstrates the point being made, so National Savings products generally deserve a mention in *The Bad Investment Guide.*

National Savings have now launched their own cash mini ISA which meets CAT standards. This has a variable rate. There is also a TESSA-only ISA available for those with a matured TESSA.

Tax Exempt Special Savings Accounts (TESSAs)

TESSAs were launched by John Major in his first and only budget as Chancellor in 1991. That was a time of historically high interest rates and at their peak TESSAs paid out 15% pa. So a 40% taxpayer could see a very real tax saving of 7.5% pa on an initial deposit of £3,000 and a maximum of £9,000. TESSAs grabbed the attention of financial journalists and we were all told that everyone should have a TESSA.

The reality was that the returns fell dramatically in line with general interest rate reductions until by early 1998 new TESSAs were offering 6.5%–7% with the new savings rate of 20% applied to the interest. For a 'savings rate' taxpayer the much heralded tax saving scheme saved them tax of just 20% of 7%, ie just 1.4% pa, which on the initial investment of £3,000 amounted to just £42 in the first year and, of course, to be enjoyed the funds had to remain lodged for five years.

Clearly a 40% taxpayer saved double that amount, but the maximum amount of £9,000 was somewhat low for many investors, so I point out to readers that here is another example of an investment scheme which disappointed many, although it did have the benefits of safety and simplicity and instant access. As an IFA I could only marvel at the number of non-taxpayers I met, including pensioners on modest incomes, who had been 'sold' TESSAs by their friendly bank or building society.

At the time of writing many TESSAs are offering 6% variable and significantly few fixed-rate TESSAs are available and those few that are offer about 6.25%. Some TESSA providers are reducing the interest paid to very low levels indeed – sometimes up to 2% less than that offered on its replacement product, the ISA. Certain financial journalists have expressed the opinion that this policy is simply to increase profits as there is no real incentive for product providers to be seen to be offering good TESSAs when the current one matures. Readers should check the rate of interest carefully. If it is too low then consider not making any further payments in, or perhaps switch to a better TESSA provider.

It therefore seems that TESSAs are not an attractive proposition at all, but readers can make up their own minds.

TESSAs linked to stock market performance

A few product providers offer TESSAs linked to the performance of the London Stock Exchange. They generally offer:

1. no risk of loss of original capital;
2. a guaranteed minimum rate of interest, usually about 5%, often some-what less than that available on normal TESSAs;
3. no income paid out, but all rolled-up;

4. an additional 'bonus' linked to the growth in the FTSE 100, which is sometimes capped.

For risk-averse investors who did not need any income and could tie up some funds (usually for five years) and who preferred the risk-free opportunity of earning additional returns, these TESSAs offered a way forward. The restrictions had of course, to be accepted from the outset. Now that TESSAs are no longer available this information is provided for the benefit of readers holding these products which may have up to five years until maturity.

PEP transfers

Although the sales of new PEPs were not possible after 5 April 1999, existing PEPs remain in place with the same savings tax benefits and CGT benefits as before, except that the decision of the Government to restrict the tax credit on dividends to 10% (referred to above) means that the savings tax benefit of equities in PEPs is halved and that small tax savings will only remain for five years.

Investors with PEPs continue to have the right to remain invested with the same manager or to transfer their holdings to another PEP manager. Investors should, as part of the sensible monitoring of all of their investments, check up on the performance of their PEPs. Monitoring may prompt a decision to transfer all or a single PEP or, alternatively, a course of action might be suggested by a financial adviser in order to:

- Move to a better performing fund
- Consolidate several PEPs into one PEP holding
- Spread investment risk
- Adopt a revised investment strategy (eg switch to a income-orientated fund)

However, readers need to be aware of the possible implications of such a move. First, the whole of a PEP must be transferred not just a part of it. Second, a single-company PEP cannot be transferred into a general PEP or vice versa. Third, and possibly the most important factor, is that the majority of PEP managers lumped PEP subscriptions into one PEP 'account' which means that they are probably unable to transfer separate PEPs effected in different years. Therefore, it is an all-or-nothing decision and all PEPs with a manager must be moved together. This can be a real snag if you want to move just one underperformer.

Any readers considering arranging transfers themselves and all advisers making such a recommendation to transfer a PEP should be aware of the following points:

- Exit charges and any other costs involved in a transfer
- The initial start-up charges (the bid-offer spread)
- Whether a single PEP or all PEPs held are included in the transfer
- Possible loss of income or growth, due to a market rise, while the PEP transfer is effected. Some PEP managers take their time dealing with transfers out.

Although those more experienced readers will have assessed the reasons for the transfer, eg underperformance, those who receive such advice from an adviser need to make certain that a convincing argument has been put forward to justify the advice. Suppose that a PEP investment of, originally, £6,000 has grown to £10,000 and the initial charge is 5%. That will extract £500 from the fund and needs to be made up before the investor can hope to see any improvement. I am generally in favour of getting out of poor performing investments but PEP transfers need care, hence their inclusion in this book.

6 Are Investment Risks Worth It?

The previous chapters attempt to set out some of the dangers and risks attached to 'risk-free investment'. The risks are mainly linked to inflation, lack of growth and falling/poor levels of income, plus the possible lack of any tax breaks – risks which are very real indeed.

It is therefore necessary to look at the alternatives available for those who will accept, to some degree at least, that the points being made may apply to them and want to make their money work harder.

The only real alternatives available are to consider investment in the Stock Exchange, either by buying shares (equities) directly in individual companies or using some sort of collective investment scheme – such as a unit trust, an OEIC or an insurance company's life fund – or to invest in property. The latter is covered in Chapter 18.

General considerations

The first general point, which must be stressed, is that asset-backed investments do contain the real risk that the capital value and income may fall and that investors may not get back the amount originally invested.

Furthermore such investments may well need a degree of 'management' coupled with having to deal with rights issues, scrip issues, scrip dividend offers, company takeovers, capital reorganisations etc. While many are favourable to investors, some may become concerned at the volume of mail and concerned at their abilities to deal with matters soundly. Most of these issues simply disappear if a collective investment scheme is used.

As a result, anyone considering asset-backed investment(s) for the first time needs to be satisfied that such investments are suitable for them. To this end, it is appropriate to try to quantify or assess the benefits that may be gained and to weigh those against the investment risks and the degree of 'management' which may be needed.

Past performance

The usual starting point in assessing the possible benefits is to look at past performance over differing timescales. While there is no doubt that past performance is no guarantee of future performance, it is the best place to start.

There is a mass of data available to demonstrate just how well asset-backed investments have performed over many years. Naturally, past performance is not all steady growth upwards but is punctuated by periods of low growth, sluggish growth, falling prices, volatility and uncertainty.

As an IFA, I kept a general file to demonstrate past investment returns for differing periods, the previous five, ten, fifteen years and much longer back to 1945, 1918 and indeed the turn of the century. The overall picture really leaves no doubt that those who have risked some of their funds in asset-backed investments have done very much better than any realistic alternative. Of course, some periods of (say) five years have done much better than others. However, the plain fact is that those who placed their money in individual company shares have, generally speaking, done incredibly well provided they were sensible, chose the companies wisely and spread their risks. Some who invested in Polly Peck, Maxwell Communications and Queens Moat Hotels lost every penny when the companies folded.

However, to paint the general picture first. Those who placed some of their money in unit trusts in the UK Equity Income sector achieved returns of 9.7% and 10.5% over the last five and ten years respectively. That total return comprises income available plus capital growth. An initial investment of £1,000 had grown to £2,748 after ten years with all income re-invested. For those readers not used to comparing investments this way it is necessary to explain that the only real way to compare investments is to look at total return available had all income available been re-invested. Of course, many holders would have had the annual income paid out to them. The system does, however, mean that comparisons can be made between a higher income plus lower growth orientated investment and another which aims for greater capital growth albeit with a lower or even a non-existent annual yield.

Reverting for a moment to the ten years' growth mentioned above, it is also relevant to mention that over the same ten-year period the annual yield/income has generally trebled. It is interesting to probe and to analyse these figures a little deeper and to separate the capital growth from the income and income growth. Below is a table showing the performance of a Schroder Income unit trust.

Schroder Income Unit Trust – Income Units

Year	Offer	Bid	%Change Year to Year	Net Income Paid In Pence Per Unit	% Change in Total Income Year to Year
	pence per unit, as at 1st Jan each year				
1985	127.6	120.0	____	5.27	____
1986	149.4	140.5	17.08%	6.10	15.75%
1987	193.5	182.0	29.54%	8.91	46.07%
1988	222.5	209.2	14.95%	8.34	−6.40%
1989	232.1	218.5	4.35%	9.92	18.94%
1990	274.5	258.1	18.23%	12.40	25.0%
1991	233.0	218.5	−15.34%	11.86	−4.35%
1992	249.0	233.5	6.86%	12.01	1.26%
1993	249.6	276.2	18.29%	12.17	1.33%
1994	391.7	367.2	32.95%	13.34	9.61%
1995	356.7	334.4	−8.93%	15.17	13.71%
1996	417.1	391.0	16.93%	16.91	11.51%
1997	467.3	438.1	12.02%	18.72	10.68%
1998	552.9	518.4	18.33%	18.79	0.41%
1999	543.6	509.5	−1.72%		

Source: Schroder Unit Trusts Ltd. June 1999.

Holders of these units in 1985 who still held them in 1998 have seen their income paid increase from 5.27 pence per unit to 18.79 pence per unit – an increase of 356%. In that time the units have increased in price by 427%, which gives a total annual return of around 14%.

The next step is to compare the results for actual income and capital growth, possibly using the annual growth rates (AGRs) from *Money Management*, with deposit-based investments and the benefits are self-evident.

A further step is to consider how inflation has eroded the value of money over the same ten-year period by applying the yardsticks set out earlier and then the overall position becomes clear.

At this stage it may be desirable to pause and consider how typical the last ten years may have been and whether some longer periods should be taken into account. It is generally accepted that the last ten years have been very favourable for investors, particularly as they now exclude the effect of 'Black Monday' in October 1987. Some readers will remember those three dramatic days when the world and UK stock markets all plummeted by alarming amounts.

The UK market fell by about 25% in two days, which shook investors rigid. However, most of the lost ground had been made up by Christmas 1988 (some 15 months later) and now the 'crash' of 1987 appears as a small blip on the graph of the rise of the FTSE (see Appendix 1).

The example used in the table is just one sector of the unit trust categories. Other sectors are available, as are other collective investment schemes (eg insurance company life funds, investment trusts and OEICs) plus direct investment into the stock exchange, all of which historically produced greater or lesser returns with greater or lesser risks attached. The point being made here is that, historically, asset-backed investments have produced good returns to investors far in excess of bonds (eg gilts) or cash/deposits and so reinforces the comments made in the opening paragraphs.

Asset-backed investments are not for everyone

Some people cannot cope with any risk and uncertainty, they are much happier with a passbook which shows to the penny exactly how much they have. To some, the concept of having only a scrap of paper evidencing units or shares with a variable value and uncertain income is wholly inappropriate, however attractive the future benefits could be. This is not to imply any criticism, but merely to state a fact of life.

It is the experience of the writer, and probably most other advisers and experienced investors, that new investors are shocked when shown the results obtained from asset-backed investments and just how well they have performed over the medium term. Nevertheless, there are many for whom such investments are just not suited and who would be well advised not to commit any of their savings into this area.

Investment risk is closely linked to time

Readers who take a few moments to consider the results of asset-backed investment over both recent years and longer timespans will soon see that the UK and world stock markets move in cycles. There are periods of high growth and periods of low growth or recession coupled with uncomfortable periods of volatility. These are often referred to as 'bull markets' (high growth/rising prices) or 'bear markets' (no growth/falling prices). There are also periods when markets just seem to mark time with little real growth. This occurred in 1991 and 1992. However, what stands out very clearly is no matter how far back one looks – 1900, 1945, or 1980 – every peak has always been exceeded.

In other words, the longer the view that can be taken, the more the investment risk is reduced. It also follows that it is only prudent to retain adequate funds in deposit-based investments so that an investor is rarely forced to sell an investment at a bad time when either the stock market as a whole is depressed or when the price of a particular investment is low. By always retaining adequate 'cash' investments, risk is much reduced.

Essential questions for investors

- Do I want my funds to be invested to aim to match inflation?
- Do I want to aim for capital growth?
- Do I want to see a real increase in my income as the years pass?

Of course the answer to all three questions is likely to be 'yes' but the following issues have to be tackled:

- Can I accept that there is some risk to some of my capital?
- Can I accept that there is some risk to income levels?
- Can I cope with some additional paperwork and the need for some on-going 'management'?
- Can I handle the added tax problems, although these may in fact be minimal, depending upon how the investments are set up?

Clearly few of us actually welcome risk and few welcome additional risk and paperwork, so new or prospective investors should, at this stage, weigh up for themselves if the possible rewards/benefits outweigh the risks and other disadvantages. This has to be a personal view. I have no doubt that provided the investments are sensible and suitable, and that the time horizons are long enough, the benefits outweigh the downside. But every reader must decide for themselves.

Re-cap for new investors

New investors should review the following:

- Past effects of inflation (see Appendix 4)
- Past record of income received from deposit based savings

and compare that with:

- The actual long-term growth of the FTSE 100 and connected investments
- Long-term income growth which has been achieved, as demonstrated by the Schroder Income Fund on page 23. Data on some other funds, to support this contention, are set out in Appendix 2

Readers should then decide if asset-backed investments appeal to them, even if only for part of their funds.

Broad historical comparisons

There is so much historical data available it is not easy to select which data to include. Readers will have seen newspaper articles and received mail evidencing massive growth over various periods of time. It is better to adopt a more cautious approach and instead look at average growth over differing periods. Some individual shares have made fortunes for lucky investors, while others have barely kept pace with inflation. Others have been spectacular disasters – remember Polly Peck? Since I expect that the majority of new and prospective investors will prefer to spread their investment risk using a collective investment scheme, probably a unit trust, the starting point is the actual returns over the last five and ten years.

Average Unit Trusts	5 Years	10 Years
UK All Companies	15.5%	10.8%
UK Equity Income	14.8%	11.2%
USA Equities	21.4%	15.6%
European Equities	16.8%	13.2%
Global Growth	10.6%	9.6%
Japan	−4.9%	−0.1%
Average Investment Trusts	5 Years	10 Years
UK General	15.4%	12.5%
European (General)	17.3%	12.8%
International General	15.0%	13.7%
Japan	−4.8%	4.6%

Source: Micropal. August 1999.

All these figures are averages and within each category some funds have performed much better. These figures are AGRs (average growth rates) and include both income available and capital growth – the total return. Sensible investors understand that it is the total return that really counts. Bear in mind that the capital growth will probably be tax free, certainly up to the current annual CGT allowance of £7,100 pa.

For longer periods various charts and graphs are included in the appendices. The trend is clear – asset-backed investments seem to increase in value as the years pass. Every peak has always been exceeded.

Spread risks

The dangers of having all of one's (investment) eggs in one basket have been touched on earlier. Although the wisdom is self-evident, the matter is worth considering in some depth because the investment scene can change quickly and sensible investors want to be able to switch at least some of their investments to take advantage of such changes.

In March 1991, interest rates were then very high with building societies paying up to 14% pa. Inflation too was high at 8.2% and the stock market was flat with the FTSE 100 at around 2,450. Guaranteed income bonds were paying out about 11% net for five years fixed. Over the next two to three years everything changed to an astonishing degree. Interest rates fell steadily (perhaps not that surprisingly) by about half to 6%. Inflation also fell dramatically to about 3% and the FTSE 100 about trebled to its present level of 6,500! Guaranteed income bonds are now scarcely attractive yielding 4% net and annuities have suffered dreadfully.

Now some of these events were predictable in 1991, particularly the fall in interest rates, if not the magnitude. The growth in the UK stock market could not have been foreseen. The withdrawal of the UK from the European Monetary Union in mid-1993 was a major factor. The resulting decline in interest rates triggered a massive rise in the price of gilts with a corresponding fall in yields. All this meant that those investors who chose to keep all of their funds in deposit-based savings lost out every way.

- They received no income growth, only a massive reduction
- No capital growth
- Few tax benefits

On the other hand, those whose who accepted some risk and placed funds in asset-backed investments have seen.

- Real income growth. The average asset-backed investment has at least doubled over the last five years
- Impressive capital growth of at least 50% over the last five years and up to 100% in USA and Europe
- Useful tax breaks if PEPs have been used to 'shelter' investments

It is fully accepted that there have been some risks along the way but the degree of risk was always controllable by simple means of careful investment selection, coupled with controlling the amount of investment capital placed at risk. The arguments in favour of asset-backed investment seem clear.

The spread of risk can also be quantified by allocating assets in the following broad categories:

1. Generally risk-free
2. Very low risk
3. Low risk
4. Medium risk
5. Higher risk
6. Very high risk

It is worth looking at the past performance of a few higher risk investments over a five- and ten-year period.

	5 Yr AGR	10 Yr AGR
Unit Trust – Aberdeen Technology	38.7%	26.8%
Unit Trust – Fidelity European Opportunities Fund	17.8%	14.7%
Unit Trust – GA North American Growth Fund	32.5%	23.0%
Investment Trust – F & C Enterprise	35.3%	25.4%
Investment Trust – Edinburgh US Tracker	21.6%	17.4%

Source: Micropal. August 1999.

It must be stressed that these funds are included here as an example of very good performing funds with track records in excess of ten years. They produce little or no annual income, but those who have commited a reasonable amount of their capital have enjoyed spectacular gains.

Geographical considerations

Most investors place all or most of their asset-backed funds in the UK for all the obvious reasons and I do likewise. However, the fact remains that the UK is not always the most rewarding area for investors as the previous figures clearly show. Indeed, over the last five and ten years both the USA and Europe have performed approximately 50% better over both periods. That is a lot of additional investment growth. A significant point to be made by *The Bad Investment Guide* is that those with sufficient investment capital should at least consider placing some of that capital in overseas equities, almost certainly via a collective investment scheme. This is likely to imply a reduction in immediate income but that is more likely to be made up by increased capital growth. The amounts invested are best quantified as a percentage of total investment capital, say, 5%–10% in both markets.

Investments in the UK stock market

Investments can be effected in the categories on page 28 or by broader sections such as smaller companies, property, financial etc.

Many investors will prefer not to follow this route and rely instead on a fund manager by selecting a good performing unit trust, investment trust or life fund, but the opportunities are there for those who are drawn to this type of investment. The risks are higher but so are the rewards. Direct investment into shares requires a wide knowledge of the matter coupled with the willingness to devote sufficient time. The topic of direct investment is covered in Chapter 14.

7 The Need to Monitor Investments

The need to monitor investments is self-evident. I hope that the previous chapters have shown this to be essential with regard to deposit-based investments as well as asset-backed investments, and more than ever to individual stocks and shares.

In recent years there has been a marked trend for banks and building societies to close accounts to new money and then open a new type of account instead. Often, the rate paid on the closed accounts was allowed (or was a deliberate policy) to fall below the going rate for that type of account. In order to increas profitability this device relied upon investors' ignorance or inertia. This practice provoked much adverse comment in the financial press and has now led to a change in practice whereby banks and building societies should notify investors of interest rate changes and the often better alternatives available. Although things have improved, the problem is still there. Some National Savings products become unattractive for the same reason. The lesson to be learnt here is that from time to time investors should take a few moments to establish exactly the returns being paid out on all such accounts, including National Savings, and then compare them with the terms generally available.

The Personal Finance Section of the *Daily Telegraph* on Saturdays only (and other papers) includes a helpful schedule of all rates of interest currently on offer from a range of banks, buildings societies, National Savings and other similar investment products. This is particularly useful at the time of writing as several life insurance companies, and some supermarkets, have set up their own banking divisions. These offer attractive rates usually based upon offering a very limited range of services typically with no cash handling, with all withdrawals being made electronically to a nominated bank account.

Fixed deposits/local authority loans/guaranteed income bonds

By definition it is difficult or impossible to encash such investments prior to their maturity dates. Nevertheless most investors would at least like to be aware of how competitive such investments remain, so it is a good idea to review these at the same time.

Investments which can be realised subject to a penalty

When the investment scene changes rapidly or the investor's circumstances change it is often desirable to realise an investment even if a penalty has to be paid. Sometimes such penalties reduce over the life of the investment, others remain at the same level until maturity, enquiries need to be made. Prior to 1999, there existed a type of PEP where returns were linked to stock market levels and which guaranteed no capital loss at maturity (usually a five-year term). However, good investment growth in 1995–98 meant that holders were showing reasonable gains and so to encash early implied no financial penalty (except, of course, the loss of PEP status of the capital).

If it becomes necessary to raise cash it may be worth considering paying a penalty attached to a poor performing investment and so leave a better performing one intact.

The main point to make here is that the implication of penalties needs to be thought through carefully and all options considered.

The monitoring of asset-backed investments

This is not as easy a task as with deposit-based investments and access is needed to share prices, unit trust prices and comparative figures. Many investors lack the time, knowledge or inclination to get to grips with it and so little monitoring ever takes place.

One solution is to find a stockbroker or IFA who is willing to undertake the task on a regular basis of at least twice a year, although more often is desirable. Stockbrokers usually charge a fee for this service, typically about 1% of the portfolio. That can seem a lot, but within my experience it only requires just one good investment decision a year to be made (which would otherwise not be made) to make the fee good value.

Some IFAs will offer this service. A fee may be payable, but it also depends upon their individual level of authorisation as not many are authorised to handle and manage individual stocks and shares. So if stocks and shares are held it is important to make sure that the chosen IFA is sufficiently authorised, otherwise the only way forward is a stockbroker (who is unlikely to be interested in offering this service for portfolios below £75,000).

In monitoring investments it is most important to remember that it is relative performance and not absolute performance that counts. If at the end of a bear market (such as 1994), when investments all fell by an average of 10% pa) one's investments were all down approximately 10%, it would be sensible to think that one had 'followed the market' and done no worse. On the other hand, to have been down by 20% would have been a cause for concern. The same attitude should be applied to favourable market conditions. If over a given period of, for example, five years an investment or portfolio has appreciated by 50% the investor may well feel pleased. However, if over the same period the stock market generally, as measured by the FTSE 100 Index or the FTSE All Share Index, has doubled then the portfolio has underperformed.

Underperformance, when compared with a suitable index, may not point to poor investment management. If an investment or portfolio contains a large proportion of low-risk investments such as with-profit bonds, distribution bonds or a cautious managed fund, then it is bound to limit upward movements and fully justifies the cautious nature of those investments. Equally when there is a general fall in stock market levels one would expect similar low-risk investments to show a much lower reduction in values.

This actually works. On 9 July 1998 the FTSE stood at 5,900. Just two months later on 4 September it had fallen to 5,175 – a reduction of 13% which was unwelcome to say the very least. However, my own holding in Sun Life Distribution Bond (a low-risk investment) fell by just 4.6%, thereby clearly demonstrating its low-risk nature. Of course when stock markets shine, that bond's performance may seem a little sedentary but it's all about matching investments to needs and attitudes to risk, both with regard to individual investments and to the overall risk profile of a portfolio. Incidentally, over the same two-month period my holding of capital shares in Schroder Split Funds plc (a very high-risk investment) fell by a massive 40.5%. The amount of money at risk in the latter was much less than the former and the high-risk nature was well understood and accepted from the outset.

The monitoring of unit trusts and life funds is fairly easy. That is achieved by buying a copy of *Money Management* which is issued monthly and provides all the necessary data on past performance to enable a view to be formed. It lists the date of launch, current buying price, fund size, yield, distribution dates and performance over periods from one month to ten years and provides a ranking in each period. Helpfully there appears, on the right-hand side, AGRs for both five and ten years and a figure for volatility. Also included are Micropal's star ratings which are an additional useful investment tool in highlighting the better and poorer funds. A quick glance along the data shows the winners and losers and which funds have demonstrated a consistently good track record over the last ten years.

A word of warning is needed. Fund managers can and do change, investment policies can alter and funds can be amalgamated, so it may be a little unsafe to assume that performance of ten years ago is a good pointer to how the fund is performing now. Many investment groups and individual funds can go through a poor period and then recover and go on to produce above average returns.

It would seem that consistency is a major factor when either picking a new fund or assessing current performance. A poor performer over the past five to ten years may now be a leader – its ranking over one to three years may be good and the reasons for the poor performance of ten years ago easily explained. In 1997–99, stock market conditions changed and some previously top-performing funds seem to have lost their way. I personally prefer bigger funds, say in excess of £100 million. Newer and smaller funds may do better in the short term but I feel that the risks are greater.

Having looked at the past performance of one's funds, most of us would like to see ours in the top quartile all the time. However, if some drift into the second quartile, that may be acceptable. But any fund which languishes consistently in the bottom quartile should be switched, unless one can see real evidence of an improved performance.

Once under performance has been identified, an investor has three options.

1. Take the hard decision to encash that investment, which may include accepting a loss and also the likely cost of switching.
2. If an improvement can be detected, defer a decision but continue to review regularly.
3. Do nothing.

Switching funds in a unit trust or a life fund usually means accepting that the bid/offer spread will remove roughly 5% from the investment which is unwelcome, but a good performing fund can easily make that up in a short time.

If a switch into a better performing fund can be achieved within the same investment house, the bid/offer spread may well be totally avoided (except for stamp duty). In addition, some IFAs are willing to share some of their commission with their clients which would reduce the cost of switching. Some capital investment bonds offer a free switching facility, or possibly offer one free switch per year with subsequent switches costing around £20. This facility is often held up as a major advantage of this type of investment over unit trusts. For readers who may be puzzled by this, switching in this context means the ability to switch all or a number of the underlying units held between different life funds run by one life office. A holder could take the view that he wanted more exposure to equities and so instruct the life office to switch funds out of their managed fund and into their equity fund.

Deciding to defer action may be sensible provided that future performance is monitored regularly and performance improves sufficiently. Matters may resolve themselves, but simply doing nothing is unlikely to be a good course of action and unlikely to make the most of your financial resources.

Monitoring individual stocks and shares

This section continues to deal with the need to monitor investments in individual stocks and shares and does not set out to discuss the merits/risks of shares in individual companies. That is covered in a later chapter.

Monitoring the price of most individual shares is not difficult. Provided that they are quoted on the London Stock Exchange, they will appear daily in newspapers. Share prices of some of the smaller companies may only be quoted in the *Financial Times* which also covers some overseas stocks. There are a range of problems associated with investing directly in overseas companies which is outside the scope of this book.

Many readers will have holdings in the privatisation issues of the 1980s and 1990s and also in the de-mutualised building societies in more recent times. Nearly all such issues have produced stunning growth, plus spectacular dividends for the original investors. It is possible that little action may be needed.

However, the matter cannot be dismissed quite so easily. At the time of writing, one power-generating company seems to be under a bit of a cloud. The share price of Halifax plc has recently been very volatile. Some depositors suddenly found themselves with one single shareholding worth approaching £10,000 and now yielding a very meagre 2.4%. There must be many shareholders in Halifax, possibly elderly pensioners, for whom a single investment of that amount and yield is inappropriate. They would be better served re-organising their investments to spread the risk and also (if required) increasing their income.

The performance of all shares should be monitored. The shares in our biggest companies such as BT and all the components of the FTSE 100 are unlikely to go bust, but readers should be fully aware that stock markets are volatile and sectors can go out of fashion, lose favour and as a result the share price can underperform the rest of the market. Conversely, some sectors come into favour and the share prices of such companies can appreciate very rapidly. In 1998 and 1999 this occurred dramatically in respect of banks, oils, pharmaceuticals and telecommunications. Any dramatic movements in share prices either upwards or downwards needs to be investigated and could be a signal to sell all or a part of the holding for the reasons set out earlier.

As an IFA, I was regularly asked to see elderly clients and advise on their investments generally. In many instances I came across individual share holdings, which had often been held for many years, in just one or maybe two companies where the high share price and valuation came as a pleasant surprise to the holder who had simply no idea of the current valuation. In many such instances the clients had previously been adamant that they were risk averse, but had to be told gently that that they currently had overly large holdings in just one or two companies and as a result were taking quite undue investment risks. In many cases income yield had fallen to very low levels and yet the clients had complained of lack of income which could be improved by re-arranging investments (subject of course to CGT constraints).

Reviewing the progress of individual shares together with all other investments is best done regularly, maybe quarterly, coupled with a note of the FTSE 100 Index on each occasion. That way, if the FTSE falls or rises significantly over any period, one can expect the performance of investments to move similarly, including unit trusts and life funds.

Of course the movement of individual share prices is influenced by market sentiment towards that company and the area in which it operates, together with its profits earned and dividend policy and the outlook for that sector.

The point to stress here is the need to monitor all your investments and to be fully aware when they perform well or perform badly! (To stay with successful/winning shares and sell losers is not a bad rule!)

At this stage refer back to my Rules of Investment in Chapter 2.

RULE 4 **Review investments regularly.** Monitor the performance of your investments regularly and take positive steps to deal with changing circumstances.

If investments perform well, prices rise and total value increases. Consideration should then be given to selling or reducing the holding in order to:

- Reduce the size of the holding, thereby reducing investment risk should the price fall back.
- Consolidate/realise gains.
- Utilise your annual capital gains allowance (more on this later).
- Possibly take the option to increase income if required.

It would not be too difficult to write a book on the topic of those companies whose share price had rocketed followed by a collapse and sometimes liquidation. Remember Polly Peck, Maxwell Communications, Queens Moat Hotels. All were large, well known companies. Of course they were somewhat exceptional. It is rare for a FTSE 100 company to go bust, but equally I could provide a long list of large companies, some with well known names, whose share price is well below that of five years ago. Many shareholders will be nursing substantial losses. In a number of cases, the writing was on the wall and sensible investment policy could have included the decision to sell at least a part of the holding to reduce investment risk.

A lady client was widowed at the age of 60. Her late husband had been a senior executive in a public limited company involved in road haulage. He had amassed a large shareholding in just that one company which now amounted to about 80% of her total resources. It seems that on his death bed his lasts words to her were 'never sell those shares dear'. I was asked to advise and had little hesitation in recommending the sale of a major part of the holding to reduce investment risk. I fully accepted the emotional attachment to the holding and recognised importance its importance to her by suggesting that she retain a significant stake. She was reluctant to take any action so the matter was referred to stockbrokers who very strongly recommended a sale of the full holding, even though CGT would be payable. It was an inherently high-risk share in a high-risk business but she could not bring herself to take a decision at all. Sure enough, the company ran into difficulties. The share price collapsed and has still not recovered after four years. A sad little story but included to illustrate the point.

8 Living with Investment Risk

Life is full of risks. I remain convinced that the most risk-averse investors who leave every penny in deposit-based investments take risks, not of losing any money but of the risks attached to inflation as explained earlier.

Some may say that Index-Linked Gilts and Index-Linked National Savings are near enough risk-free and provide inflation-proofing. There is some truth in that and there are investors who may feel content with that option. However, two points need to be made.

1. Index-Linked Gilts and Index-Linked National Savings pay out a very low income indeed, currently about 3.5%.
2. With the RPI at about 3% and likely to go lower, total return is very low and it should be possible to better it.

For those reasons I suggest to readers that there are still some investment risks here, hence their inclusion in *The Bad Investment Guide.*

Many popular Capital Investment Bonds and Guaranteed Income Bonds are single premium life policies so the Policyholders' Protection Act of 1975 provides very substantial cover against the failure of the issuing life office and thus that risk is virtually eliminated. Furthermore, many hold the view that the Government would be very reluctant to see a life office fail and would in all probability mount a rescue operation.

All other investment vehicles contain risk. Risk is hard to define and to measure but it's a bit like toothache – when its there you know about it!

Categories of investment risk

Many investment advisers and companies issuing investment products sometimes categorise investment risk in bands from very low risk to higher risk. The following table is my own construction and so readers may feel inclined to amend the categories to meet their own investment ideas and standards.

Generally risk-free	Bank/building society accounts National Savings products Guaranteed income bonds Guaranteed growth bonds UK cash unit trusts
Very low risk	Cautious managed unit trusts Cautious manager life funds With-profit bonds Gilts (short term risks only) UK gilt funds Zero-dividend preference shares
Low risk	Some balanced managed unit trusts Some managed life funds Most distribution bonds Global Equity and Bond funds Global Bond funds
Medium risk	Managed unit trusts Managed life funds Shares in general investment trusts
Higher risk	Equity unit trusts Smaller Companies' unit trusts and investment trusts Equity life funds Individual company shares
Very high risk	Some individual shares Some single country funds Emerging markets funds Warrants and options

The same data and the same concept are set out another way in a 'staircase of investment risk' in Appendix 7. Many new or first-time investors are able to relate to that chart and find that it can be helpful in formulating their investment policy. Some unit trust companies categorise their funds on the same basis as the above table.

Quite a good way to plan your investments, get to grips with investment risks and control your own degree of risk is to place all existing or proposed investments into the six categories quoted (although some readers might wish to reduce the number of categories).

Applying this principle the following is a suggested spread for differing types of investor:

	Totally risk-averse	Very low risk	Low risk	Medium risk
Bank Building Society a/c National Savings	100%	60%	40%	20%
With-Profit Bonds		15%	10%	10%
Distribution Bonds		10%	15%	15%
U/T Managed Funds		10%	15%	10%
Equity U/T and Life Funds		5%	15%	20%
International U/T			5%	15%
Single Country Funds Emerging Markets Individual Stocks and Shares				10%
	100%	100%	100%	100%

These percentages are a suggested level and individuals should set their own. The point to be made here is that by having an investment strategy from the outset it is possible to manage your investments more successfully, and both in good times and poor times you are more likely to have your overall finances better arranged. If some investments perform well and appreciate, that strategy could lead to a reassessment and to taking profits and rearranging investments in the manner suggested earlier.

During 1995–99 there have been some dramatic increases in share prices generally and some unit trusts. Of course, not all shares have done well. Banks, oils, pharmaceuticals and more recently telecommunications have produced some startling gains. Some investors are now holding very unbalanced portfolios and the arguments in favour of taking profits are strong. On the other hand, funds investing in some single countries and in emerging markets have generally had a torrid time. While I am rarely in favour of single country funds, the emerging markets sector is now much stronger and there may be a case for adding to investments in that area. The whole point is that the system provides an overall framework to work within and will enable investors to be fully aware how the investment scene may have changed and prompt appropriate action.

9 Unit Trusts and OEICs

Unit trusts and OEICs (Open-Ended Investment Fund Companies), together with life assurance funds, are the principal collective investment schemes open to investors in the UK. Investment trusts are similar in many ways but there are important differences, so investment trusts are considered separately in Chapter 11. For the purpose of this book space is not taken to outline all the features of unit trusts. That is already dealt with elsewhere and many readers will have a knowledge of the matter.

This is a big investment area indeed. At the present time there are approximately 150 management companies managing some 1,700 funds valued at £209 billion.

Readers will be aware of the general principle that unit trusts, and all other collective investment schemes, 'pool' the collective savings of numerous investors and then manage them in accordance with the stated aims of each fund. The individual investors are not necessarily 'small' investors. Many wealthy people may prefer to use unit trusts than to invest directly into the stock market.

In setting the scene for this chapter, it is necessary to explain that unit trusts are a UK concept. In the USA they are known as 'mutual funds'. There is no real equivalent in Europe which means that they cannot easily be marketed or promoted there because of their legal status and structure. The financial services industry wishes to expand into Europe which is one of the reasons why management companies are converting from their unit trust status into OEICs. Existing unit holders are not affected by this change and in practice there is little real difference. The principal difference is that whereas unit trusts always had two prices represented by a bid/offer spread, under OEICs there is just one price, which of course reflects the value of the underlying assets.

When a new investor buys units in an OEIC the contract note has an extra item added to the purchase cost which reflects the initial charge and includes any commission payable to any intermediary. This change in practice is also supposed to make matters clearer for investors.

The aims and objectives of all investment funds (and life insurance funds) will be clearly set out in key features documents, fact sheets, managers' reports, booklets and other publications issued by management companies. Broadly, these aims and objectives will include:

- The emphasis on income or on capital growth
- The nature of the underlying investments, eg equity, general or smaller companies
- Geographical nature, eg UK only, Europe, USA or International
- Specialised market sector, eg mining shares, technology stocks
- Degree of risk undertaken, eg recovery stocks, FTSE 100 stocks only

The unit trust sector is split up into performance categories introduced and monitored by AUTIF (Association of Unit Trust and Investment Funds). Those categories change from time to time to reflect general changes in the investment scene. The present categories are listed below.

Income funds with an 'immediate income' objective

UK Gilt Funds

Funds which invest at least 80% of their assets in UK Government securities (gilts).

UK General

At least 80% of the trust's assets must be invested in corporate or public fixed-interest securities.

Global Bonds

At least 80% of their assets must be invested in fixed-interest securities. Most funds in this sector contain a spread of Government and other fixed-interest securities from all over the world and are managed to take advantage of varying interest and currency rates between the different economies.

Managed Income

Contains at least three asset classes, but no more than 60% can be invested in equities. The fund must aim to have a yield of at least 120% of the FT All

Share Index gross yield before charges. At least 50% of the fund must be in Sterling/Euro and equities are deemed to include convertibles.

UK Equity and Bond Income

At least 80% of their assets must be invested in the UK, with between 20% and 80% in UK fixed-interest securities (bond income) and between 20% and 80% in UK equities. These funds aim to have a yield in excess of 120% of the FT All Share Index. The fixed-interest element means that these funds are often able to provide a relatively good level of income and offer more security of capital than an equity fund. Balanced funds usually aim to provide a combination of income and growth. Some funds are managed to provide especially high levels of income, some use derivatives to convert future capital growth into income. These give the option to maximise income by giving up some opportunity for growth.

Funds with a 'growing income' objective

UK Equity Income

Funds which invest at least 80% of their assets in UK equities and which aim to have a yield in excess of 110% of the FT All Share Index. Managers of these funds seek out UK shares of companies in a broad range of industries with yields that are above average compared with UK shares in general. They select shares of companies which they believe will be able to pay steady or increasing dividends in the future. Capital growth is not a priority, but in the past equity income funds have tended to produce good levels of capital growth as well.

Global Equity Income

At least 80% of their assets must be invested in equities and which aim to achieve a yield in excess of 110% of the FTSE World Index. Overseas shares tend to pay lower dividends than UK companies, but this sector includes funds that specialise in higher yielding, international shares to cater for investors who seek income.

Growth funds with capital growth/total return

UK All Companies

At least 80% of their assets must be invested in UK equities which have the primary objectives of achieving capital growth. Some funds invest in a variety of companies whose share prices the fund managers believe are likely to grow strongly. Some might invest in a range of companies of different sizes in different industries. Others might specialise in the shares of large 'blue-chip' companies. Some funds aim to mirror or 'track' the progress of the UK stock market as measured by a specific index, such as the FT All Share Index. The manager may achieve this by buying the constituent shares or by investing indirectly via futures and options.

UK Smaller Companies

At least 80% of their assets must be invested in shares of UK companies which form part of the Hoare Govett Smaller Companies Index or have an equivalent or lower market capitalisation. These funds are generally considered to be of higher risk than funds which invest in companies of varying sizes.

Japan

At least 80% of their assets must be invested in Japanese securities.

Far East including Japan

At least 80% of their assets must be invested in Far Eastern securities including Japanese. However, the Japanese content must make up less than 80% of assets.

Far East excluding Japan

At least 80% of their assets must be invested in Far Eastern securities excluding Japanese. This includes funds investing generally throughout the Pacific Basin, including Australian and New Zealand securities.

North America

At least 80% of their assets must be invested in North American securities. Most funds invest in a broad range of US and Canadian companies.

Europe including UK

At least 80% of assets must be invested in European securities. They may include UK securities, but these must not exceed 80% of the fund's assets.

Europe excluding UK

At least 80% of their assets must be invested in European securities and exclude UK securities.

Cautious Managed

Investments are made in at least three asset classes, with the maximum equity exposure restricted to 60% of the fund. Assets must be at least 50% Sterling/Euro and equities are deemed to include convertibles. These funds are a natural progression from a bank or building society account into the stock market.

Balanced Managed

Contains at least three asset classes, with equities limited to 85% of the fund. At least 10% must be held in non-UK equities. Assets must be at least 50% Sterling/Euro and equities are deemed to include convertibles. Investors who want more than a bank or a building society account can give, might find these funds attractive.

Active Managed

Offers investment in a range of assets, but up to 100% of the fund can be invested in equities. In addition, at least 10% must be held in non-UK equities. There is no minimum Sterling/Euro balance and equities are deemed to include convertibles. At any one time the asset allocation of these funds may hold a high proportion of non-equity assets. However, the funds would remain in this sector since it is the manager's stated intention to retain the right to invest up to 100% in equities.

UK Equity and Bond

At least 80% of their assets must be invested in the UK, with between 20% and 80% in UK fixed-interest securities and between 20% and 80% in UK equities. These funds aim to have a yield of up to 120% of the FT All Share Index. The fixed-interest element means that these funds are often able to provide a relatively good level of income and offer more security of capital than an equity fund. Balanced funds usually aim to provide a combination of income and growth. Some funds are managed to provide especially high levels of income, some use derivatives to convert future capital growth into income. These give the option of maximising income by giving some opportunity for growth.

Global Growth

At least 80% of their assets must be invested in equities which have a primary objective of achieving growth of capital. Included in this sector are funds investing in a spread of international blue-chip companies.

Global Equity and Bond

Between 20% and 80% must be invested in fixed-interest securities and between 20% and 80% in equities. The investment objectives of these funds are similar to UK Equity and Bond funds except that they can invest in all the major markets of the world.

Global Emerging Markets

Trusts which invest 80% or more of their assets directly or indirectly in emerging markets as defined by the World Bank, without geographical restriction. Indirect investment, eg Chinese shares listed in Hong Kong, should not exceed 50% of the portfolio. The funds in this category typically invest in rapidly developing economies, and are generally considered a higher risk investment than those exposed to more established markets.

Property

At least 80% of their assets must be invested in property securities. There is little actual investment directly held in property.

Growth funds with a 'capital protection' objective

UK Money Market

At least 95% of their assets must be invested in money-market instruments (ie cash and near cash, such as bank deposits and very short-term fixed-interest securities). They offer a way for small savers to get 'wholesale' rates of interest and at the same time retain easy access to their money. As the capital value of money market funds is unlikely to change, and in some cases is actually fixed, these funds may be an attractive supplement to a bank or building society account for savings set aside to meet short-term needs, but not everyday spending requirements.

Guaranteed/Protected Funds (other than money market/cash funds)

These aim to provide a return of a set amount of capital to the investor, with the potential for some growth.

Growth specialist funds

Six sectors are subdivided by the geographical location of the underlying investments. These sectors incorporate funds which do not fit comfortably into other sectors. They can include funds concentrating on a single country (eg Korea), or a single theme (eg ethical) or a single sector (eg healthcare).

UK Specialist	*Japanese Specialist*
North America Specialist	*Far East Specialist*
European Specialist	*Global Specialist*

Pension funds

These are only available for use in a personal pension plan or FSAVC scheme. Present arrangements for unit trust personal pension schemes require providers to set up a separate fund under an overall tax-sheltered umbrella. These funds in turn invest in the group's equivalent mainstream funds. Pension funds are not to be confused with 'exempt' funds which are operated mainly for institutions.

Index Bear funds

These are designed to track the performance of an index by using derivatives and are only suitable for people prepared to accept a high level of risk.

Sector classification

Note: In June 1999 AUTIF revised and changed the sector classification system for unit trusts. This was a very fundamental revision and some sectors which had been in place for many years, such as 'UK Income and Growth', totally disappeared. As some readers will recall previous categories, or indeed see them referred to in previous publications or investment recommendations, it is helpful to include a full list with sector definitions as has been included above. These changes are beneficial and describe the objectives of each sector in a much clearer way.

Sectors and performance

It has to be made very clear that although all are unit trusts the differences between the sectors is very great. There is a world of difference between a Global Bond fund and a Global Emerging Markets fund. Indeed the difference is not unlike the difference between a sports car and a van. Both are suited to different needs, have little in common, but provide transport. There is a totally different emphasis on income generation vis-à-vis capital growth and the degree of risk and volatility are also different. Both may well good investments but for quite different people with differing investment aims.

Within each sector there is then a massive difference in the past performance of differing funds. Indeed, those past track records can vary so widely that consideration of past performance is a major feature of this book.

A problem for existing holders of unit trusts is to be aware of just how well or how badly their funds have performed. Most readers will be aware that investment performance is all about relative and not absolute performance. If over any given period your unit trust has gained in value by, for example, 10% you may feel that that is good or at least satisfactory. However, if the sector overall gained by 15% then clearly your fund has underperformed by a massive 50% – the reverse also applies.

The only way to assess past performance is to obtain a suitable publication such as *Money Management* which provides very comprehensive past performance statistics. Interpreting that data is vital for those investors who wish to really assess the performance of their unit trusts.

Throughout the financial services industry, one key measure of success is quartile ranking. This is just what it says and any similar group of investments such as unit trusts, life funds or pension funds are divided up into performance over a specified period and shown in four quarters. Most fund managers strive to achieve top quartile rankings and that is seen as a major mark of investment management success. Quartile ranking is even more important because is it used as a measure of assessing the investment performance of fund managers when overall assessments are made periodically of unit trust management companies and pension providers

It is self-evident that however well a fund manager does, only 25% can ever be top quartile and so to be second quartile may be seen as a good performance. A fund can just miss the top quartile over a number of timescales and still claim a good performance. It is often worth looking at individual rankings carefully to see when a fund is placed in a quartile. The presentation of the data makes that relatively easy. Although top quartile ranking is often the aim of both fund managers and investors, there are other yardsticks which are almost as important and should, I believe, be considered along with quartile rankings:

- Volatility
- Consistency of performance
- The size of the fund and time since launch

Volatility

The extreme right-hand column in *Money Management* assesses volatility. The importance of this factor is a matter for the individual investor to decide. However, most investment advisers would say that good performance with low volatility must be better than the same performance with high volatility. Volatility is another way of looking at investment risk. If a fund manager is taking risks in the pursuit of success that may show up as an above average level of volatility. Put another way, an unusually high level of volatility could be a warning of above average risk.

Consistency of performance

Consistency of performance really speaks for itself. Reviewing past performance means looking at all the data. Over a relatively short period of two or three years a very small fund may have done well, but many advisers look for a larger fund with a long track record, in excess of ten years, and judge consistency that way.

Funds and fund managers may change! The standard risk warning attached to all regulated investments is that 'past performance is no guarantee of future performance', and that must be right. However, past performance will be what most advisers and investors look at first. It is important to be aware that a fund may have changed direction at some stage or that the fund manager may have changed, so past performance may be totally irrelevant.

However, most sensible investors have to start somewhere and a careful look at *Money Management* data would show that a high level of good consistency simply has to be a plus point compared with a consistently poor performance. Some investment houses seem able to demonstrate a high level of consistency which may be a pointer to generally sound fund management.

Occasionally, a unit trust fund changes its emphasis or, more likely, the manager, which results in a dramatic improvement in performance. The result can be that a dismal performance over the previous five to ten years is then replaced by top quartile performance over the short term. Similarly, when previously good above-average performance suddenly ceases, advisers and investors are quite entitled to ask why. When that happens, or if such a fund is recommended, it is always possible to ask an adviser or indeed the management company for an explanation. On several occasions as an IFA, I was faced with such a situation and every time the management company, when asked, provided a detailed explanation for the situation, usually coupled with an outline of steps taken to correct matters.

A very useful set of figures in *Money Management* which appears in the right-hand columns are two columns which show AGRs (annual growth rates) over the last five and ten years. A glance at the same figures for the sector averages shows how well or badly a fund has performed over two reasonably long periods of time. Clearly no comparisons are possible until a fund has been running for five years.

The size of the fund and how long it has been running

As an IFA I preferred to place clients' money into larger funds, generally those over £100 million. I was always reluctant to support very small funds. A bigger fund can spread risks higher and can generate sufficient fee income to support a better level of investment expertise than a little fund of £2 million. It has to be said that the smaller funds should have the ability to outperform the very large ones. This area has to be a matter of personal preference.

New funds can sometimes perform very well over the first couple of years. They start off with a 'clean sheet' and can invest initially in all the best areas. They will simply not have to live with mistakes or the problems of changes in stock market fashions. On the other hand, when picking unit trusts as an IFA, I tended to look at performance over the last ten years and then work backwards in time and form a view of past performance and consistency that way.

Over the last 15 years or so the unit trust industry in the UK has done well for its investors when based upon AGRs and total returns compared with the alternative, which for most people would have been to leave the funds in deposit-based savings accounts.

Action based upon past performance

Having looked at past performance of existing units trusts most investors will reach the following conclusions.

1. The fund is doing well and no action is called for.
2. The fund is seriously under-performing and should be disposed of.
3. While performance has been disappointing there are now signs of improvement so the matter must be watched to see if the trend continues.

Sometimes performance is just so poor that the decision is easy. One problem for many investors is that having identified underperformance there is the understandable reluctance to do anything positive about it. As a result the underperformance continues.

Coming to a decision to part with any poor investment is never easy and to switch always costs money. To switch unit trusts will usually take about 5% off the capital but that can be a price well worth paying to get better performance. If you can switch to another fund with the same fund manager the bid/offer spread can be avoided. At least the move away from the traditional unit trusts to OEICs may make this step less expensive.

Making sure that your unit trusts are in the right sector

Although this seems a very obvious consideration, I am sure that there must be very many holders of unit trusts who, for one reason or another, are holders of units which are not appropriate to their needs. This goes back to my earlier remarks about the need to review investments carefully and regularly.

To take an extreme case, someone could be holding units in a Smaller Companies fund, an Emerging Markets fund or a European Equities fund, some or all of which could be top performers. But, if the need now was to maximise income, all of those could be inappropriate and possibly a Corporate Bond fund or a UK Equity and Bond Income fund might be more appropriate to their needs. The investor's age will also figure in the assessment of suitability.

Some investors are in the comfortable position of not needing to maximise income; a reasonable return will suffice. For them, a Corporate Bond fund, offering no chance of income growth or of capital growth could be the wrong choice and instead an UK Equity and Bond fund could prove a much better choice ten years later!

Index tracker funds

These unit trusts set out to 'track' a particular index instead of being actively managed. They are promoted and marketed on the basis that numerous fund managers fail to match the performance of the FTSE Index and that managed funds carry heavy, relatively high, management charges. Index tracker funds are not actively managed as such and therefore annual management charges tend to be less. At the time of writing there has been a maximum of only five years' past performance figures available for a few tracker funds. About 18 funds now have three years' past performance figures. Those years in which index tracker funds have been in existence have seen favourable stock market conditions which have, of course, benefited tracker funds. Their performance has been excellent, leading the supporters of the concept to claim it as a total success. However, in my opinion it is far too soon to be so certain of the long-term success of the concept and it will be necessary to see how trackers will fare in adverse stock market conditions.

It is desirable to sound out a note of caution on trackers at this stage while in no way seeking to disparage past performance. One problem with these funds is that they must by definition 'track' the index to which they are connected. During 1998 and 1999 there has been an explosion in the share prices of some shares, particularly telecoms and internet stocks. Take Colt Telecom as a specific example. This company has never made a profit and achieved sales of less than £250 million yet currently has a market capitalisation of £8 billion and is on a high price/earnings ratio of 32. Tracker funds have had to buy these shares, which are tightly held, therefore pushing the price even higher.

Active managers, who aim to pick the best stocks, might well feel that such shares are simply too expensive and do not offer value and/or that the high price might contain an overly high level of investment risk. The managers of the tracker funds claim that this concern is unfounded and that the spread of risk is sufficient to meet the risks. Part of an active fund manager's job is to diminish investment risk by controlling the exposure to any one company or sector of the market.

It is now claimed that about one-third of occupational pension schemes now use index tracker funds, but the extent of their members' investments is far from clear. It seems to me that there must be a case for investors carefully considering the use of tracker funds as a part of an overall investment plan. The performance of tracker funds varies considerably as the table overleaf shows.

While performance varied greatly, out of these 18 funds no less than 15 were in the top quartile over the one year to 6 June 1999 and the remaining three were in the second quartile. Interestingly, in the year to June 1996, which is outside the three-year period of this table, eight out of the nine funds in existence were in the bottom quartile. New funds with a very short track record over only one year have been omitted from this table.

The concept of index tracker funds is not limited to the UK market and numerous overseas markets can be tracked. In fact, over the last year to June 1999 those who had funds in USA trackers, together with World Indices and Japan, all did considerably better than UK trackers. Only European trackers fared worse. This seems to be a powerful pointer in support of an opinion expressed much earlier in this book in favour not having all of one's investments linked solely to the UK stock market and the UK economy.

How FTSE 100 Tracker Funds Performed – Gains on £1,000 Invested over 1, 2 and 3 Years
(Offer to bid, net income re-invested)

	One year	Two years	Three years
FTSE 100 Index	83	372	703
CF netPEP Tracker	106	392	— —
Direct Line	99	425	827
Scottish Widows	96	418	— —
NatWest	84	392	— —
Guardian	100	408	— —
Fidelity	107	429	848
River and Mercantile	95	375	765
Marks & Spencer	95	411	809
HSBC	87	395	798
Legal & General	83	376	756
CGU	70	372	— —
Midland	43	334	713
Equitable	51	354	727
Mercury	38	330	684
Barclays	34	329	684
Lloyds TSB	31	326	704
Sovereign	57	311	677
Govett	8	317	628
Average	**71**	**372**	**741**

Source: Micropal. August 1999.

Investment risk

There is a real danger that some newer investors who have invested in tracker funds may underestimate the degree of investment risk. There is an argument that a FTSE 100 tracker fund is not low risk at all. The reason is that it is so dominated by a small number of core companies. A setback in one large sector, eg oil shares or banking, could have a disproportionate effect on the unit price. No one could seriously claim that a Japanese tracker fund was low risk!

Conclusion

The concept of tracker funds is still relatively new and they are vehicles which have enjoyed very favourable investment conditions. Many first-time investors will have been attracted into trackers by a combination of excellent marketing, low charges and short-term good investment performance. There is now clear evidence that very large amounts of institutional portfolios in the UK have transferred from actively managed funds to index trackers. That amount could be between 15% and 20% of such institutional funds, which includes pension fund assets. It seems that there is now a case for private investors deciding to include tracker funds alongside managed funds in their own portfolios.

10 Single Premium Policies or Bonds and Life Assurance Funds

Most but not all life assurance companies provide facilities for the investment of lump sums in much the same way as unit trust management companies. However, this type of collective investment scheme is different because the result is achieved by the investor buying units in a single premium life policy. The whole of the premium (the initial lump sum to be invested) is used to purchase units, although an initial charge of around 5% may be included in the price of the units in much the same way as with a unit trust.

Nearly all of the units are of the accumulating type which means that all the income generated goes into the life fund, together with any capital gains on dealing. All add to the value of the fund and therefore the price of the units. There is rarely any stated or quoted 'yield' or return.

Investors can at the outset select a suitable fund to meet their investment aims – such as an Equity, Smaller Companies, Property or European Smaller Companies fund. The categories are very similar to those on pages 42–47 which apply to unit trusts.

Although there is no stated rate of return, income is available by encashing units regularly which can provide an income paid monthly, quarterly, half-yearly or yearly. The way that income is paid can be easily varied by merely instructing the life office by letter.

Tax considerations

There is a long-standing 'concession' whereby annual withdrawals of up to 5% of the initial sum invested may be made free of income tax. This is a much used and convenient method of generating income, but various points need highlighting.

1. The life fund itself has already paid income tax on the fund income so the 5% 'concession' has already suffered some tax.

2. Non-taxpayers cannot recover the tax already paid, so generally speaking

these bonds have hitherto not been suitable for non-taxpayers who would have been better served investing in unit trusts where tax deducted at source could easily be reclaimed annually. That difference changed with effect from April 1999 after which non-taxpayers can no longer reclaim 'tax credits'.

This point is somewhat complicated and so non-taxpayers need to exercise additional care when investing in order to minimise any income tax paid.

3. Withdrawals in excess of 5% pa are possible but that may erode capital.

4. Withdrawals in excess of 5% pa lead to a 'chargeable event' and the life office must advise the Inland Revenue. This is no problem for basic rate taxpayers but may lead to an additional tax liability for higher rate taxpayers.

5. When the bond is eventually sold, or if any lump sum withdrawals are made, both transactions are 'chargeable events' and may lead to an additional tax charge in the hands of a higher rate taxpayer. This is a complex area and any higher rate taxpayer needs to take specific advice on this point before making any lump sum withdrawals or total encashments.

6. The income tax treatment can work to the advantage of higher rate taxpayers. Funds invested this way are taxed within the fund. If no withdrawals are made at all the investor can defer either taking an income or encashment until after retirement when his or her top rate of tax may fall to the basic rate. This is really a part of standard financial planning.

7. One major benefit of these bonds applies when holders have no need for any immediate income. All income in the bond accrues and there is no paperwork to be included in annual income tax returns.

8. For the above reason, investment into this type of bond appeals to trustees. This point is covered in Chapter 20.

9. One tax disadvantage of these bonds compared with unit trusts is that they do not enjoy the CGT exemptions that are available to unit trust managers.

Claimed or perceived advantages of unit trusts

The above points mainly relate to the tax position. There are other advantages and disadvantages compared with unit trusts. Needless to say their veracity depends very much on the person you talk to. Unit trust managers are apt to claim that their product is better and are quick to quote the advantages listed below.

1. The CGT exemption they enjoy when capital gains are made within the unit trust fund itself.

2. Initial commission paid to advisers is usually lower, typically 3% for unit trusts compared with, typically, 5.25% in the case of life funds. There is some truth in this. However, many IFAs are willing to rebate some of their commission back to clients which can lead to an additional sum being invested.

3. Unit trust management companies like to claim a higher degree of expertise in running unit trusts than that on offer in life offices.

Claimed or perceived advantages of the life funds

1. The ability for investors to be able to 'switch' all or a part of the investment between differing funds in order to meet changing investment aims or to increase/decrease investment risk (eg Balanced Managed fund to an Equity fund or vice versa).

2. The ease of starting, stopping and changing income withdrawals.

3. Some of the income tax advantages as set out above.

It does seem that on carefully examining the actual past performance figures in *Money Management* that over the longer period unit trusts do appear to perform slightly better than the life funds. However, the advantages set out above will be a major consideration for some investors.

Distribution bonds

These are a special type of insurance life fund and have been a very popular and successful form of life fund since the idea was 'invented' by Sun Life in 1978. Some investors have never liked the concept of encashing units to provide the '5% tax free' annual income because the number of units held decreases constantly.

As a result, Sun Life designed a modified type of bond whereby the income accruing was placed in a separate fund and paid out regularly as income and the number of units remained unchanged. The income could always be left in to maximise growth and a variable income could always be paid out. The initial investment policy of the Sun Life Distribution Bond was very successful indeed. It was low risk and set out to appeal to risk-averse investors and to outperform building society/deposit-based savings. That good investment performance is reflected in both income and capital growth. Now numerous life offices have launched their own distribution bonds but the underlying investment spread can vary considerably. Some include property in their funds whereas others do not. A table of the past performance of the Sun Life Distribution Bond is included in Appendix 2, partly in order to demonstrate its success and in addition to emphasise the overall success of asset-backed, low-risk investments.

Readers who wish to take a close interest in their investments can of course see the breakdown of the fund from Key Features Documents (KFDs) and other published data. Typically there is a high level of investment in gilts and/or other fixed-interest securities to increase the income stream and also to reduce risk.

The relative performance of all distribution bonds can be found in the appropriate section of fund analysis in *Money Management.*

With-profit bonds

This is yet another type of insurance fund which has much in common with the general distribution bonds and insurance funds described previously. The one major difference is that the value of units should not, under normal circumstances, fall.

With-profit bonds were first marketed after the stock market 'crash' on Black Monday in October 1987 following investors' general reluctance to place money into asset-backed investments which contained risk.

A new type of life fund was launched into which investors could buy units at the market price. Those units (in a unitised life fund) then increased exactly in line with that life office's with-profits reversionary bonus rate, meaning that the rate of annual bonuses were added to their with-profit life policies.

At the time of launch and for some years after, those bonus rates were high. Those funds therefore attracted a huge level of support and were widely promoted by the life offices and widely recommended by advisers.

The important thing for readers to grasp is that with-profit bonds are really very low risk indeed. The unit price can never reduce (clarified later) but the chances for capital growth are also limited. Remember that the units in a managed fund or an equity fund can move upwards or downwards without limit.

Whereas in insurance funds generally the units are unlikely ever to be worthless they can fall dramatically in any stock market downturn. They can also move upwards significantly in time of stock market boom. So units in with-profit bonds cannot fall below the purchase price but the upside is limited.

The low-risk nature of with-profit funds, coupled with their stated aim of out-performing building society returns, means that they have very wide appeal to investors. The 5% pa, tax free, annual income availability is the same as the general type of bonds described previously. At the time of writing, the 1999 bonus rates are being declared and the average seems to be about 5.8%. The steady reduction in interest rates generally, which seems likely to continue, means that these low-risk bonds offer the prospect of reasonable returns.

Some past performance figures are now becoming available. For the last three and five years the seven best performing with-profit bonds have produced average compound returns of 8.14% and 8.6% respectively. So those investors who withdrew the usual 5% still have around 3% pa of growth left in.

With-profit bonds sometimes offer the prospect of terminal bonuses after funds have been invested for at least five years. The rates of return currently quoted may be lower in the future.

In line with current returns, however, not all with-profit bonds have done well. As with all other investment products discussed in this book, the annual bonus rates, terminal bonuses and charges all vary considerably. The poorer-performing companies are unlikely to admit that their products have poor performance. There is a problem with performance comparisons because, for technical reasons, past performance figures are not regularly available in *Money Management* in the same way as unit trusts, life funds and pension funds. One benefit of dealing with an IFA is his or her ability to access this comparative data and so recommend a good product. For readers who wish to do their own research in this area there are three options:

1. ask a friendly broker or IFA to provide data for you;

2. search out the periodical survey of Planned Savings in *Money Management* or similar publications;

3. obtain an independent survey available either free or at modest cost.

With-profit bonds risk

In this section I have referred to with-profit bonds are being almost risk-free. There are in fact three areas of risk.

1. The annual bonus rate is not fixed or guaranteed and may reduce. However, they are unlikely to reduce greatly.

2. The life office may fail. This is again a remote risk. Should that occur, then there is the protection available under the Policyholders' Protection Act 1975.

3. The application of the Market Value Adjuster (MVA). Almost all with-profit bonds include a market value adjuster in the small print. This unwelcome but necessary provision is included to protect remaining investors should some wish to cash in their bonds at a time when the stock market is or has been falling rapidly and the with profit-fund needs to liquidate stock quickly, thus possibly incurring losses or expenses. These could either be borne by the fund, in which case existing investors would suffer, or be passed on to those generating the cost, namely investors withdrawing from the fund. MVAs are designed to protect the fund for the benefit of existing investors. In a 'Survey of With-Profit Bonds' by *Money Management* in December 1997, it listed 23 product providers of which nine guaranteed not to apply an MVA on tenth-year anniversaries. The number drops to two for fifth-year anniversaries. Only eight companies have applied MVAs within the last six years.

Some companies guarantee not to levy an MVA in the circumstances of a bond being encashed on the death of a holder; others guarantee not to apply an MVA in instances of regular withdrawals.

While the inclusion of the MVA is unwelcome, there is really no alternative in the interests of all the investors in a life fund. The scenario demonstrates the general merit of spreading investment risk and not having too many eggs in one basket, in this case to avoid having to encash a with-profit bond at the wrong time, which might trigger the application of the MVA.

11 Investment Trusts

Investment trusts are not really trusts at all but joint stock, limited liability companies whose share price is quoted on the London Stock Exchange. Its issued share capital, as with all such companies, is of a fixed amount and for this reason investment trusts are sometimes referred to as 'closed-ended trusts'. Additional capital can of course be issued from time to time subject to the normal company procedures for doing so.

Unit trusts, which are trusts set up under a trust deed, are often referred to as 'open-ended'. That means that if the managers receive an application to buy units they simply issue or create new units to match the amount to be invested. So the implication and use of the term OIEC will now be clear!

Investment trust companies do not trade or carry on a business of any sort. They just invest the shareholders' funds in other trading companies in a similar way that unit trusts for life funds do. However, there are several technical differences between investment trusts and unit trusts and each category must be considered separately, but first a little more general background is needed.

General background

Investment trust companies were first established in the nineteenth century with the aim of offering investors of moderate means the same advantages as larger investors by pooling their money together. That principal remains today. Investment trusts invest primarily in the shares of other companies. Each trust has a well spread portfolio of investments, run by professional fund managers and supervised by an independent board of directors. Investment trusts offer an easy way into the stock market. There are a wide variety of trusts to meet different investment needs in much the same way as exists with unit trusts. Today there are over 300 investment trusts with combined assets of around £65 billion. Investments trusts are separated into categories on similar lines to unit trusts.

International General

General investment trusts with less than 80% of their assets in any one geographical area.

International Income Growth

General investment trusts with less than 80% of their assets in any one geographical area, whose policy is to accentuate income growth.

International Capital Growth

General investment trusts with less than 80% of their assets in any one geographical area, whose policy is to accentuate capital growth.

UK General

Investment trust companies with at least 80% of their assets in UK registered companies.

UK Capital Growth

UK specialists with at least 80% of their assets in UK registered companies whose policy is to accentuate capital growth.

Endowment Policies

Investment trust companies that invest at least 80% of their assets in with-profit endowment policies of life assurance companies.

UK Income Growth

UK specialists with at least 80% of their assets in UK equities, excluding convertibles, whose policy is to accentuate income growth.

Commodity and General

Investment trust companies with at least 80% of their assets in listed commodity and energy shares.

High Income

Investment trust companies with at least 80% of their assets in equities and convertibles which aim to achieve a yield in excess of 125% of the yield of the FTSE Actuaries All-Share Index.

North America

Investment trust companies with at least 80% of their assets in North America.

Far East excluding Japan

Investment trust companies with at least 80% of their assets in Far Eastern securities, which exclude any Japanese content.

Far East including Japan

Investment trust companies with at least 80% of their assets in Far Eastern securities, which include a Japanese content of less than 80%.

Japan

Investment trust companies with at least 80% of their assets in Japan.

Property

Investment trust companies with at least 80% of their assets in listed property shares.

Europe

Investment trust companies with at least 80% of their assets in Europe.

Emerging Markets

Investment trust companies with at least 80% of their assets in emerging markets.

UK Smaller Companies

At least 80% of the investments trust's portfolio will be invested in the shares of UK registered companies and 50% by value of the portfolio invested in the shares of smaller and medium-sized companies.

Smaller Companies International

At least 50% of the value of the trust's portfolio will be invested in the shares of smaller and medium-sized companies.

Closed-Ended Funds

At least 80% of the assets invested in other investment trusts and other closed-ended investment companies.

Venture and Development Capital

A significant portion of the investment trust company's portfolio is invested in the securities of unquoted companies which are subject to directors' valuations. Due to the cost of valuing unquoted shares and the time involved some choose not to value assets on a monthly basis. Where this is the case, net asset value/net asset value total return figures will not be shown.

Split Capital Trusts

This is a complicated area of investment and is dealt with later.

Source: AITC July 1999.

Investment trusts and capital gearing

A major feature of investment trusts and one that differentiates them from unit trusts is their ability to borrow money. As well as equity capital, investment trusts almost invariably have preference or debenture stock, which provides an element of gearing to the benefit of ordinary shareholders in times of rising market prices. As one of the prime objectives of investment trusts is to increase the capital value of the ordinary shares, it is important to appreciate the relevance of gearing.

Explanation of gearing

Gearing in a conventional investment trust relates to the effect of borrowings or prior charges. An investment trust can borrow money – and use it to buy other assets. If the total assets grow in value, the shareholders' net assets grow proportionally more, because the debt stays the same. Gearing is not without some risk in adverse stock market conditions. An example will help:

An investment trust has the following capital:

£5 million in debenture stock
£10 million in ordinary shares

It is to invest £2.5 million in fixed-interest stocks and £12.5 million in equities.

Suppose that the value of the equities rise by 20%.

Value of funds invested in equities would then be	£15m
Add value of fixed-interest holdings	£2.5m
	£17.5m
Deduct value attributable to debenture holders	£5.0m
	£12.5m

So, an increase in the value of the equities to the extent of 20% has increased the assets attributable to the ordinary shareholders by 25%. Similarly, if all of the funds had been invested in equities, the benefit of the rise to the ordinary shareholders would have been 30%.

On the other hand, if £5 million of the funds had been placed in fixed-interest stocks then the capital gearing would have been neutralised. Readers will easily see that the position works in reverse and that a 20% fall in the underlying assets will cause more than a 20% fall in the ordinary share price the higher the level of gearing.

It follows that anyone considering placing funds into an investment trust would be wise to at least consider the level of gearing. Many investment trusts take advantage of their ability to borrow and to 'gear up'. The level of borrowing and the amount of 'gearing' varies considerably and seems to be on average about 15%–20%. If the fund managers invest well and/or stock market prices rise then such investment trust shares should outperform, but clearly the risks are greater.

The effect of charges

All collective investment schemes levy charges as they are expensive to run. Good fund managers can command high salaries in addition to the potentially high costs of research and investment analysis. Put another way, no one will undertake to manage funds on a full time day-to-day basis for nothing. This applies to unit trusts, investments trusts and life funds.

Unit trusts tend to levy an initial charge of around 5% when funds are first invested, but it can be up to 6%. There is then an annual management charge of 0.75%–2% with the average at about 1.5%. The charges on life funds are similar. By contrast, investment trusts have always claimed to have much lower charges in general. Shares purchased directly from the managers suffer no initial charge and if bought through a stockbroker will suffer the usual stockbroker's charge of around 1.85% plus stamp duty of 0.5%. The annual management charges on investment trusts are often less than 0.5% of the total assets.

The unit trust movement tends to claim that total charges are not so great and that investment trust managers are prone to conceal charges within the accounts of the investment trust in a way that unit trust managers cannot. I have always taken the view that provided good investment performance is achieved by the managers, I am not too concerned at the level of charges. If poor performance is delivered, that could be a significant ground for switching the investment.

The effect of charges may be more significant when considering investments into a UK gilt or fixed-interest fund or into a Corporate Bond fund where the degree of 'management' should possibly be less. When investing clients' funds as an IFA, I looked for lower charging unit trusts within these categories.

The importance to be attached to charges is a matter of personal choice and something that individual investors must decide for themselves.

Investment trusts and net asset value (NAV), discounts and premiums

This is another major difference between unit trusts and investment trusts. The published unit prices for unit trusts is an accurate and precise valuation of all of the underlying assets held by the unit trust. The unit price is therefore an accurate expression of the value of the unit and hence the investment.

With investment trust shares the price of the shares at any one time is the price ruling in the market, ie the London Stock Exchange. Although that price will reflect the value of the underlying securities, there is another factor, namely the stock market's view of the attractiveness of the shares. There are in turn several factors influencing the stock market.

1. Demand and supply for the shares. Remember that the supply of shares is totally fixed and so any significant increase in buyers may lead to an increase in the price and vice versa.

2. The general standing of the investment trust company and its managers.

3. The general investment sentiment concerning the area in which the trust invests. A specialised trust or one linked to a geographical area will be influenced (for better or worse) by the sentiment for or against its area of operation, be it Commodity and Energy, Emerging Markets or Japan.

4. From time to time investment sentiment moves in favour of, or against, investment trusts generally, which can raise or lower prices.

The difference between the underlying assets and the market price is called the premium or the discount. When the market price is below the net asset value (NAV) the shares are said to be trading at a discount and when they are above the NAV they are said to be trading at a premium.

Investment trusts' shares usually trade at a discount. The primary reason for the discount is a function of demand and supply for the investment trust's shares on the stock market. A widening discount indicates that there are more sellers than buyers. Alternatively, an increase in NAV may contribute to a widening discount. Investors buying shares at a discount are paying less than the underlying assets are worth but, once they are shareholders, they receive dividends out of the income received from the full value of those assets (less the trust's expenses and any amount retained by the trust).

A look at the history of investment trusts helps to put the discount into perspective. In the 1970s the tax regime for investment trusts and private investors investing in the stock market became particularly harsh. The supply of investment trust shares increased as institutional investors tried to sell their holdings in the face of much reduced demand. The average discount for the industry widened to more than 30%.

In the following decade, the tax regime for private investors and investment trusts became more favourable. This was followed by the advent of savings and investment schemes and later by PEPs which provided investors with a low-cost way of investing in investment trust shares. A third factor was the increase in awareness of investment trusts as the Association of Investment Trust Companies (AITC) embarked upon a generic advertising campaign emphasising the excellent performance and value of investment trusts.

Increased demand for investment trust shares led to a narrowing of discounts into single figures in the early nineties. However, it also encouraged many management companies to launch new investment trusts which in time inevitably led to over-supply, with the result that the average discount has since widened again to low double figures. It is important not to place too much emphasis on the overall average discount as this will not reflect the experience of every investment trust.

Readers will now be asking is a discount good or bad for buyers? To assume that you are automatically getting a bargain if you buy at a discount (the bigger the better), or that you are not getting value for money if you buy at a premium, is a dangerous generalisation.

It is the growth of the underlying assets that will, over time, drive the share price. As a long-term investor it is more important to concentrate upon the prospects for the underlying assets than to concentrate on the current level of the discount. When deciding what to buy it is important to match your own investment aims with that of an investment trust in much the same way as with a unit trust or a life fund. Risk must be fully taken into account, coupled with the need to construct and implement an overall investment strategy.

The most important aim will be meeting actual investment objectives of income or capital growth. For funds committed to investment trusts the primary aim will probably be capital growth. If the discount narrows during the period of your investment this is 'the icing on the cake'. It provides a proportionally better return during the ownership of that asset. A widening of the discount does not necessarily indicate a loss or a poor investment performance. There could still be a good capital gain but that gain may be said to have been reduced to the extent that the discount has widened. There could be various reasons for this as mentioned previously.

Discounts and premiums are neither good nor bad for investors. They are simply a facet of this type of investment and one which prudent investors should be aware of from the outset.

Finally on this point, although a very wide discount may be a source of irritation to holders there is nothing that they can do about it. However, the

Capital shares

Capital shares (with a few exceptions) pay no dividends. They do not have a predetermined redemption value but instead are entitled to any assets remaining at the winding-up date after other classes of shares have received their entitlements. They are last in the order of priority which makes them a higher-risk investment.

Units

Some split capital trusts have arranged for a combination of their shares to be traded together in what is known as a 'unit' or a 'packaged unit'. This is not to be confused with units issued by a unit trust.

Warrants

A number of split capital trusts have issued warrants. Warrants are not a class of share but a type of security which offers the right but not the obligation to buy shares at a specific price at a specific date or period in the future. These tend to be a higher-risk investment.

Some general considerations affecting all classes of shares in 'splits'

Risk and reward

No class of share is guaranteed a return – even those with a predetermined entitlement. The level of capital return depends upon the success of the managers in increasing the value of the assets sufficiently to repay all classes of shareholder in the trust; the level of income return depends upon the success of the managers in growing the revenue from those assets. The higher the gearing, the greater the need for the assets to perform both in terms of capital and income.

Assessing splits

There are a number of factors to take into account when assessing split capital trusts. The ratio within the trust and order of repayment will affect gearing and thus the level of risk for a particular class of share. The investment policy of the trust will affect the performance of the assets and their ability to respond to the requirements of the different classes of share. The length of time before winding-up is also important as, the longer the life, the more time the managers have to grow the assets and income of the trust.

Statistics

There are a number of published statistics relating to splits. These include figures indicating whether there are sufficient assets available to repay certain classes of share known as 'asset cover'. The rate of growth needed to achieve repayment is the 'hurdle rate'. This important investment concept is explained in Appendix 6.

Taxation

If you invest in a split capital trust and receive dividends you will be treated in exactly the same way as if you received dividends on any other ordinary shares. Higher-rate taxpayers will have additional income tax to pay. After April 1999, non-taxpayers are unable to claim back any 'tax credits', which they had been able to do previously.

Financial advice

While I have tried to explain many of the complexities of splits, it is just not possible to cover all those that may affect any individual share together with matching the needs of individual investors. Therefore, I strongly recommend that any readers who consider that investment trusts may be appropriate for them should do the following:

- Carry out more research for themselves.

- Contact AITC who issue, at no charge, a most helpful range of explanatory leaflets on all aspects of investment trusts.

- Contact an IFA who is suitably qualified to advise on investment trusts in general and on splits in particular. It should be made clear that the vast majority of IFAs and also 'tied agents' are not permitted to advise the public on investment trusts. The AITC has set up a helpline to assist investors in finding IFAs who are able to advise on investment trusts.

- Accept from the outset that this is a complex area of investment. Different classes of shares contain a very wide spread of investment risk from very low risk to very high risk and so great care is needed.

Some of the data included in this chapter was provided by the AITC to whom the author would like to express thanks. The AITC will provide, free of charge, information packs on all aspects of investment trusts and can be contacted at:

Durrant House, 8–13 Chiswell Street, London EC1Y 4YY.
Tel: 020–7431–5222.

12 Higher-Risk Investment Schemes

This chapter will briefly cover:

- Venture Capital Trusts (VCTs)
- Enterprise Investments Schemes (EISs)
- Enterprise Zone Property Trusts (EZPTs)

These three higher-risk investment schemes are examined together. Most readers will not become involved with them for two reasons:

1. the majority of financial advisers are neither qualified nor authorised to advise on these schemes;

2. their appeal to most investors is very limited, due mainly, but not exclusively, to the higher level of risk involved.

However, because of those risks and other problems they deserve inclusion in *The Bad Investment Guide*. Such schemes also warrant a mention because some readers will be aware of their existence which may be attractive and suitable for investors who:

- like to take greater risks;
- are higher rate taxpayers;
- have substantial CGT liabilities; and
- can really understand the risks and are attracted to a particular scheme.

Venture Capital Trusts

VCTs were introduced in 1995 to replace the Business Expansion Scheme (BES) and offer generous tax breaks to encourage investors to put their money into unquoted companies with the intention of helping to stimulate that sector of the economy. However, fewer than 30,000 investors have bought VCTs since their launch so it would seem that the apparent risks and/or the conditions attached have led investors to steer clear.

Readers who can recall the early days of the BES will remember the spate of optimistic investment schemes which were promoted – Angora goats, vintage cars, Australian vodka – followed by less adventurous schemes linked to residential property. Many investors lost heavily when these schemes floundered or were wound up.

In reality VCTs are a much safer investment than their name implies because of the spread of investment risk and, on the whole, may well be less risky than investing directly in a range of equities, particularly very small companies.

VCTs are quoted investment trust companies that invest their shareholders' funds in private companies or in companies quoted on the Alternative Investment Market (AIM). There are three basic tax breaks available to a VCT investor, who may place up to £100,000 during any one tax year.

1. Dividends on ordinary shares in the trusts are exempt from income tax.

2. Subscribers to new VCT shares are entitled to 20% income tax relief provided that the shares are held for at least five years, ie an investment of £80 would acquire £100 worth of VCT shares. If the shares are sold earlier then the tax relief must be repaid.

3. Investors are exempt from CGT on the sale of ordinary shares, and new subscribers may also use a VCT scheme to defer an existing CGT liability (up to a maximum of £40,000) up to the amount subscribed. Only the gain needs to be invested, not the total sale proceeds of the investment that generated the CGT liability. So a 40% taxpayer can effectively invest into a VCT and avoid/defer 60% of the initial investment – 20% of income tax plus 40% of CGT.

There is usually a spate of new VCT schemes in February and March each year as the end of the tax year approaches and potential investors effect year-end tax planning. It is probably best to regard VCT as a specialised investment vehicle with attractive tax features, rather than a tax-planning tool.

As the first VCT schemes were launched as recently as 1995, and because of the five-year rule, there is no real market yet in VCT shares and is too soon for any general pattern of investment success to have emerged. The initial growth of VCT shares has been lacklustre to say the least. However, if investment managers get it right, and investment conditions are favourable, there could be very high returns seen within a couple of years. There is now a section devoted to VCT shares at the end of the section on investments trusts in *Money Management*.

It is very important to make clear to readers that the initial tax relief of 20%

is only available to investors subscribing for new shares so it only makes sense to buy shares at a new offering. Once the initial five years is up it seems likely that the VCT shares may suffer from a general desire of the initial holders to sell, after which time those shares are likely to be viewed and valued on a similar basis as other investment trust shares which concentrate in the venture capital area. Interested investors should be aware that there are other vehicles available giving exposure to that sector.

VCTs tend to focus on smaller companies, mostly existing companies or management buy-outs, but, as mentioned previously, they can invest in unquoted and AIM companies. VCTs do offer investors the opportunity of spreading investment risk in unproven businesses, while having in-house experts to research and manage the deals.

There is a list of businesses that are excluded from participation in the VCT scheme, principally companies engaged in land, commodities, hotels, sharedealing, nursing homes, farming and forestry. That list can be amended by the Government, usually in the Budget.

The risks of investing in a VCT should not be underestimated. Venture capital is always particularly vulnerable to the economic cycle, coupled also with some political risks depending upon the extent to which the Government wishes to support this sector of the economy. It is fully accepted that this latter risk seems to be low as the present time, but it may not always be so.

As a result, investors in VCTs who shelter capital gains and other investors should ensure that VCT investments along with other moneys invested in smaller companies do not constitute too large a proportion of their portfolio. There are no rules on how many VCTs an investor can hold, but because the tax breaks force investors to stick with the funds for five years there could be a danger if investors become too heavily committed to the scheme.

That there are two distincts area where success or failure can occur.

1. The general economic climate – as with all other 'asset-backed' investments.

2. The VCT manager's skills. This is hard for investors to assess. One way is to inquire into past performance in running venture capital schemes. All managers should be able to provide figures for past performance. A further test is to try to assess the 'realisations' which the trust has made. A realisation occurs when managers sell their stake in a firm they have invested in, hoping to make a substantial profit, but sometimes sustaining a loss. Realised gains flow directly into the asset value of the trust. Check too the trust's 'deal flow'. That is the rate at which the managers have

closed new investment deals. VCT managers must have 70% of their funds invested in qualifying companies within three years of launch. If their deal flow is too slow they may find themselves rushed into poorer investments later on. Managers with good reputations tend to get offered the pick of the deals.

The British Venture Capital Association publishes regular lists of new VCT issues. They can be contacted on 020–7240–3846.

Enterprise Investment Scheme

The Enterprise Investment Scheme (EIS) was announced in the November 1993 Budget as a simplified replacement for the Business Expansion Scheme (BES) which was withdrawn. The EIS came into force on 1 January 1999. In the March 1998 Budget the EIS was merged with CGT Retirement Relief. The revised EIS is aimed at encouraging investment in new shares in qualifying trading companies. The main changes were:

1. an increase of 50% pa in the amount that can be invested, up to £150,000;

2. unlimited deferral relief from CGT for individuals and trustees where disposals are invested in eligible shares;

3. when EIS shares are issued in the first half of the tax year the tax relief can be carried back to the preceding year, subject to 50% of the amount subscribed, to a maximum of £25,000;

4. extension of the limitation on the underlying investment by the exclusion of farming, forestry, property, hotels and nursing-home companies.

The EIS comprises a series of tax reliefs, which are available to qualifying new equity investments in qualifying unquoted companies. The principal reliefs are:

• initial tax relief of 20% of the amount subscribed;
• deferment of CGT due;
• exemption from CGT, provided the investment is held for five years.

The pitfalls include a combination of higher risk and absence of liquidity, coupled with the uncertainty about the final exit routes after five years. EIS investments perhaps should be compared with a VCT, ie as a quoted company, which should mean that the shares are easily saleable. An EIS investment has no similar exit route.

Enterprise Zone Property Trusts

Enterprise Zone Property Trusts (EZPTs) were first established in 1981 to facilitate economic regeneration in areas targeted for commercial activity. To attract private sector investment, initial tax allowances of 100% are given to commercial property development in Enterprise Zones. The zones themselves benefit from a simplified planning regime and occupiers enjoy exemption from non-domestic business rates.

An Enterprise Zone Property Trust acquires commercial property on behalf of investors. Investors, in turn, acquire units in the EZPT and are entitled to tax allowances pro rata for the value of the units acquired. There is no limit to the amount that may be invested in a EZPT. It is only the size of the EZPT that ultimately restricts availability and, accordingly, most investors can normally select the number of units to match exactly their requirements for tax relief. Another feature of EZPTs is that, typically, loans are made available to enable investors to structure their investments in a more tax-efficient manner with immediate cashflow benefits.

EZPTs invest in offices, industrial, and to a lesser extent, retail property within Enterprise Zones. These properties may be pre-let or speculative. In pre-let properties, long-term tenants will have been identified prior to acquisition by the EZPT. As a result, investors often receive retail income from the properties immediately.

EZPT's can provide investors with a means of investing directly into commercial property while sheltering unlimited levels of income at the highest marginal rate of tax. Investments in EZPTs can be structured in such a way that no net cash outlay is required because, in addition to obtaining income tax relief, investors are typically offered a finance facility of up to 70% of the cost of the investment via a pre-packaged loan. In other words, the tax rebate is greater than the net investment.

EZPTs are designed as long-term investments and, in order for the tax reliefs to be safeguarded, the trust must remain in existence for 25 years. However, after seven years what is called a 'lesser interest' in the property can be sold. The amount that can be invested is unlimited; however, there is usually a minimum requirement of £5,000 or £22,000 if a loan facility is used. The tax relief available under the EZPT scheme is quite independent of the other incentives such as the VCT scheme or the EIS.

The investment risks are hard to quantify. The ultimate success of the investment will depend upon the growth and future price levels of the underlying properties, which can be subject to distortion because of the accruing tax allowances. Even ignoring that, there may be large fluctuations in prices as a result of the degree of success or otherwise of each individual Enterprise Zone. EZPT investments are intended to be held for long periods, usually 25 years, and there is no established market in which to trade them. If the underlying property is realised within seven years, there will be a clawback of capital allowances.

It is my opinion that although some pre-let schemes may be low risk, overall EZPT's should be entered into only by those with some knowledge of commercial property and who are able to evaluate the underlying properties and risks for themselves.

Overall conclusion on these three investment schemes

The complex nature of these schemes will be apparent. Readers actively considering using any one of them clearly need to take extra care and I would recommend the following as a course of action.

- Check that your adviser is authorised to advise on these schemes. Although that in itself is no guarantee of expertise or suitability, absence of an adequate level of authorisation would be a worrying factor.

- Quantify the tax breaks, both the initial income tax benefits and the possible deferment of CGT.

- Try to quantify the investment risk. In 1997 the writer suggested that a wealthy client defer a CGT liability by the purchase of shares in a local, well known but privately owned brewery. The investment risk was not perceived to be very great either by the stockbroker or by the writer. The matter did not proceed because the client could not make up his mind quickly enough and the shares were sold elsewhere. Later the same client considered a VCT scheme which involved investing in one or more sea-going vessels which would service oil rigs in the North Sea. The ultimate success of the investment really depended upon the re-sale value of the vessel(s). Here the risks seemed to be very much greater and the client decided not to proceed. I believe that this example demonstrates the point.

A special risk warning must be signed, a specimen of which is included in Appendix 8. Although these three schemes can have substantial tax benefits they should only be entered into by experienced investors and even then only after a portfolio of more conventional investments have been put in place.

13 High-Income Bonds and Higher-Income Bonds

During the period 1996 to 1999 Higher-Income Bonds were launched by some product providers, mainly insurance companies. These were single premium life policies with a life of between four and six years. They offered a very high and fixed-rate of return over the life of the investment but the final repayment of capital was always linked to the level of one or more financial indices, usually the FTSE 100 Index, S and P 500 for the Dow Jones or the DAX.

The returns offered were usually in the range of 7%–10% pa paid net of UK tax and tax-free (except for higher-rate taxpayers). The initial investment was usually at least £5,000 and income could be paid out monthly, annually or compounded over the life of the bond. There was often a 'bonus' paid for early application which was added to the capital sum at the outset or added at maturity. Such bonds are always launched in tranches and for a fixed period of between one and three months and then withdrawn. These products should not be confused with guaranteed income bonds, which generally entail much less risk.

Repayment of capital at maturity was dependent upon one or more indices not being lower than at the outset. Some, however, link return of capital to some actual growth in an index over the period, say, an average of 3% pa. As a variant some issues promised full repayment provided that, for example, the FTSE 100 had not declined by more that 15% over the period. A reduction of more than 15% would trigger a reduction in maturity proceeds. This latter variant would be likely to offer a lower rate of income to compensate for the lower investment risk.

At the time of writing one such bond is available for a four-year term which offers 7% pa tax free, equivalent to 8.75% to a basic-rate taxpayer. Return of capital is linked to the FTSE only and does not require any growth in the FTSE. Interestingly, at maturity, if the FTSE is lower then the repayment, moneys will be reduced pro rata. So, if the FTSE was to fall by 5% over the four-year period an initial investment of £10,000 would see a return of £9,500. There is a further safeguard that however much the FTSE were to drop there would be a final payout of 40% of the original capital plus all income paid out. Early encashment may be possible but is subject to penalties and to the level of the stock market to which the bond is linked.

Repayment linked to two or more indices adds to the risk. For a while the Personal Investment Authority banned such issues linked to more than one index, but the practice seems to have returned!!

Numerous sales aids have been prepared by the companies promoting these bonds, indicating that statistically the risk of the indices falling is very remote. There have been other articles in the financial press claiming that the promotion of these bonds is a 'guaranteed scandal'.

There is no doubt that there is some investment risk attached to these bonds but that risk is hard to quantify. It has been the writer's experience that some more knowledgeable and experienced investors seem quite willing to take that risk, which they perceive to be very small indeed. The attraction of such bonds is that, at the time of writing, the after-tax income is likely to be about double the amount obtainable from deposit-based investments.

Conclusions

- There is certainly some risk which investors should be aware of and set off against the benefits of the extra income to be enjoyed.

- There must be every likelihood of not having to try to encash early.

- If the investment is to proceed then the amount committed should not be too great a proportion of the investor's capital.

- Remember that if interest rates increase then the income benefit will be reduced or lost but the investment risk will remain.

- It seems better to be linked to one index rather than to two or more.

- For risk-averse investors, the type which offers a lower return, but which would pay out 100% of capital even if the FTSE 100 declined by up to 15%, could offer extra peace of mind and be more attractive.

- The level of the FTSE 100 Index (or other linked indices) at the time should possibly be taken into account. At the time of writing (also the time of the launch of the bond described above) the FTSE is at an all-time high. This does not of course mean that the investment should not proceed but it is not a helpful factor!

used have not been set out here. Those readers wishing to obtain a deeper knowledge should carry out further research in this area.

- **Current income** – as measured by the dividend yield

- **Growth expectations** – as measured by the price/earnings ratio. This is always referred to as the P/E ratio and is a major indicator of the price of the share compared with the stock market average and with other companies in its sector. The P/E ratio is such as important investment yardstick that a full description is included in Appendix 10.

- **Dividend cover** – provides an indication of possible scope for future dividend increases and in simplistic terms the higher the level of dividend cover the better.

- **Gearing** – in this context it is the total of prior charge capital and all borrowing as a percentage of the shareholders' capital. Clearly companies who have over-borrowed may have an overly large burden of debt to meet on an annual basis which could reduce their ability to pay dividends. Many large companies have little or no borrowing which can be an indicator of a strong balance sheet and have appeal to some investors. It is not possible to be too dogmatic on the level of borrowing a company can manage, but most investors prefer to see the gearing ratio no greater than 40%.

- **Net asset value (NAV)** – This was covered in the chapter dealing with investment trusts and speaks for itself. It varies greatly between companies in different sectors. Some investors ignore it completely, taking the view that with companies in such sectors as pharmaceuticals and IT it has little relevance. On the other hand, it would be a major consideration for anyone considering an investment in a property company.

Most of these mathematical measures are quoted in the financial press, although not all of the time. Some are only quoted on Saturdays or Mondays and others, such as the gearing ratio, are harder to locate but do appear in the *Investors Chronicle.* There are some small publications which deal solely with explaining these various investment ratios and measures; any reader wishing to take the matter more seriously should obtain a copy.

There are other assessments of share value but they are less exact.

- **Market capitalisation.** Is it a large FTSE 100 company or does it appear in the FTSE 250 or is its total value below that level? Most investors want to know the size of the company in which they may invest. Smaller companies generally imply greater risk and the shares of the very smallest may not be easily marketable. From time to time investor sentiment may favour bigger companies. For quite long periods the shares in all smaller companies have been out of favour. They may then lag behind market growth and offer above average scope for appreciation in their share prices.

- **Financial track record of both profits and dividends.** Many investors are in favour of companies which have a long track record of both profits and dividends. This may point to sound, steady management but remember that nearly all of the biggest companies can have a profit upset, a prime example being Marks & Spencer in 1999.

- **Share price in relation to the high/low range for the year or longer.** On its own this can be misleading, but compared with the level of the share price of similar companies may indicate that some further investigation is called for.

Selecting individual shares – building a portfolio

Many people get into share ownership by chance. They may inherit some shares or acquire shares through SAYE schemes or share options connected with their employment. Many people applied for privatisation issues on the back of heavy promotions at the time (remember Sid and British Gas!). And more now hold shares in the de-mutualised building soicieties and insurance companies. Some buy shares to obtain 'shareholder perks' and a few will buy following tips in the press which catch their eye or as a result of the remarks by a friend.

Any readers who are tempted into this very rewarding area of investment should perhaps decide at the outset what their investment aims are (income or growth) and the degree of risk they will accept, just like any of the other investments mentioned in this book.

However, there is one huge difference between direct investment and a collective investment scheme. In the former you have to manage the investments yourself and in the latter someone does it for you. As we all know, shares can go down as well as up. A familiar problem for experienced investors is that no bell rings when a share price peaks or when a trough is reached.

An attractive capital gain of, for example, 20% in a short period may be the maximum over a much longer period or if the gain is realised may look a poor decision if the share price doubles within a short time. Similarly with losses, will you sell when the share price falls by, for example, 15% or hang on for the shares to recover? If you sell and the shares fall further it is a good decision, but if they recover then it is not so good. It is often easier to lose money than to make it and care is needed.

It is highly desireable to have some knowledge of why share prices move and to be able to assess, however basically, the investment risk attached to a particular share. The main factors are listed below.

Political considerations

There can be no doubt that some governments are by their philosophy fundamentally unfavourably disposed towards private enterprise, although for practical considerations they may be prepared to allow a mixed economy consisting of both nationalised industries and private enterprise to co-exist. There may be a lack of sympathy towards private enterprise and shareholders, coupled with a harsh or unhelpful treatment of company profits or the payment of dividends or the imposition of exchange-control restrictions. Alternatively, many economies in the developed world, Western Europe, North America, Japan and the Pacific Basin actively encourage private enterprise and capitalism generally and make efforts to attract the largest multinational companies.

Economic considerations

Profits are the foundation upon which a company's prosperity rests and accordingly share prices are closely tied to the economic climate both in this country and abroad. In times of recession when business is slack it can be hard for companies to make profits. If profits are falling, or are low, then there will be insufficient cash to meet reasonable dividend expectations which will depress share prices. In addition, companies will have insufficient funds to plough back into the businesses to sustain growth.

Emotional considerations

The main price movements both upwards and downwards tend to be overdone. The reason is that investors, whether private individuals or fund managers, are not calculating machines but human beings. They are therefore influenced by the market atmosphere which they themselves have helped to create.

When prices are rising, coupled possibly by good economic news, a mood of optimism prevails. Adverse news can easily be swept aside as being of little consequence. Everybody wants to be 'in the market' and not to miss out on future rising prices. As a result the market can be talked up to unrealistic levels and become overheated. At that stage some adverse news can trigger a setback. Some readers may recall a significant fall in share prices in the early months of 1994 triggered by a small increase of just 0.25% in US lending rates, which was not unexpected.

The opposite state of affairs applies in a bear market. Prices can be falling as the result of sound reasoning but then fall to unduly depressed levels as pessimism gets the upper hand. Investors can simply stay away. A policy of high interest rates may accelerate that process.

Investment fashion

Many things in life are influenced by fashion and the investment process is not exempt. Although the majority of investment decisions will be reached after sound analysis using all the normal criteria, there are times when the rise in one sector gets overdone. The writer remembers some years ago there was a sudden awareness of environmental issues which triggered a rise in the prices of any share which could claim even the remotest link with the environment, even down to dustbin manufacturers. Eventually, investment sentiment moved on with consequent price adjustments downwards. In more recent times, the price of all pharmaceutical shares has reached very high levels fuelled no doubt by some initial sound reasoning. However, the P/E ratios now mean that new investors are paying well in advance for future growth. The biotechnology and Internet stocks are further cases in point where share prices are astronomical for companies which may never have achieved any sales nor yet made any profit!

Market rating

In most sectors there are usually a few shares that have higher P/E ratios and other investment yardsticks than others in the sector. This is usually because they have produced consistently good results over time. Such companies are said to be 'highly rated' and as a result are often the preferred choices for investors seeking safety. Readers must be aware that when fortunes change for a highly rated share, the share price can have further to fall. It may take a very long time to recover its high rating and may never really do so. BTR, Sainsbury's and Marks & Spencer provide good examples of this.

The decision to buy or sell shares and the evaluation of existing shareholdings

If readers feel inclined to buy shares for the first time (excluding applying for privatisation issues etc) what is the way forward? There are four choices:

1. seek the advice of a stockbroker, bank or other financial adviser;
2. rely on recommendations in the popular press or the more specialised publications such as the *Investors Chronicle*;
3. do it yourself relying upon your own judgment and based on your own investigations and experiences;
4. possibly a mix of the above.

Readers of this book will, I feel, be sufficiently interested to want to carry out at least some evaluation for themselves based upon all of the criteria set out previously and backed up by other reading and research. The same tests can be applied to existing shareholdings. One useful test is 'Would I buy these shares now?', coupled with 'Why am I retaining the investment?'

However, be warned that it can be an uncomfortable exercise if a holding or several holdings are looking lacklustre. Here, the same range of options applies as discussed earlier under unit trusts, namely:

1. take the hard decision to sell and (possibly) cut losses;
2. retain in the hope that the share price will recover;
3. decide to watch the position closely.

Building a portfolio (the buying decision)

This is a complicated matter which is only touched upon briefly here. Generally, most investment advisers recommend that investors embarking upon direct investment should spread their resources among at least 12 and possibly up to 20 holdings in order to obtain an adequate spread. This is to minimise investment risk and at the same time participate in investment growth across the broad economic scene. Since the minimum sum which can sensibly be invested in a single share is around £2,000 that implies having around £40,000 available.

These matters are broad pointers. Clearly you can invest lower amounts, but the minimum charges for both a purchase and a sale when applied to an investment of, for example, £1,000 means that a 10% rise in the share price will be needed to cover dealing costs. With initial stakes of, for example, £3,000 a much smaller percentage rise would show a useful profit.

Of course there is nothing to prevent an investor buying shares in just one or two companies, particularly if he/she considers them a good investment. However, it is best to keep in mind the following points.

- The price of shares can fall. If just one or two holdings are bought and the price(s) fall for whatever the reason, the investor has losses. If funds are spread across a portfolio then at any one time although one or two may have depressed prices, others may have appreciated.

- As explained above, individual shares or sectors can fall out of favour and individual shares can be re-rated downwards. If just one or two holdings are bought and suffer either of these effects there is nothing to compensate for the losses.

The London Stock Exchange divides all quoted shares into about 36 sectors covering the range of industries and markets. Some of the principal sectors are listed below.

- Banks
- Breweries, pubs and restaurants
- Building
- Chemicals
- Electricals
- Engineering
- Household and textiles
- Media
- Oils
- Pharmaceuticals

Many investors aim to cover all or most of the UK market. The amount committed to each individual share need not be the same, more could be placed in 'safer' shares and less in smaller companies or sectors, such as building, which historically are more risky.

A generally accepted and sound investment policy is that it is unwise to have more than 5% of investment capital committed to any one share. That is of course to minimise risk (Investment Rule No 2 in Chapter 2) and points to a portfolio of some 20 shareholdings. In the case of some of our biggest and soundest plcs, 10% may be acceptable but above that level the degree of investment risk is greatly increased.

However, it is probably a sound investment policy to have some exposure to the big sectors as a matter of course because they tend to dominate the economy. At the present time such sectors would comprise oil, pharmaceuticals, bank and telecom shares.

Having made investments, the problem of monitoring progress and management has been a constant theme of this book. Whether individual shares do well or do badly there is a real need for prudent investors to be aware of the position and take positive action when it is required (although very often that decision may well be to take no action at the time).

Always remember that direct investment can be undertaken alongside collective investment schemes. There is no question of it having to be all or nothing. Indeed, it is sometimes a good policy to use unit trusts alongside a portfolio of shares in order to gain access to a specialised market sector such as Smaller Companies or Emerging Markets.

Monitoring strategy

Once acquired, stocks and shares should be monitored on a regular basis (at least quarterly but more often is desireable).

- Check the share price and be aware of price changes. If they are large, try to discover why. It is always helpful to be aware if the price has moved up or down purely in line with market/sector movements or if other factors are at work.

- Read the financial press for news of your companies in particular and the sectors in which they operate. Good or bad news for a sector will effect most companies to some extent.

- Read the company's reports – never an easy matter! They are of course designed to paint the company in a favourable light but some useful pointers may be gleaned. It is one area where gearing is usually shown. Most companies now include a table showing the key performance figures of turnover, profits and dividends over the last five years. Depending on the nature of the business, that can be a useful pointer to consistency.

- Note carefully any significant changes in the P/E ratio. These are a pointer to the market's view of that company.

- Be aware of profits and losses. I have long been in favour of minimising losses and realising at least some of the profits.

- Share prices can move upwards and downwards very quickly in response to good and bad news. In such periods it is only sensible to watch the price more often. If in doubt as to whether it is prudent to buy or sell some or all of the holding it can only be helpful to have access to an adviser.

15 Investing in Gilts

Introduction

Gilts are marketable securities issued by the British Government when it needs to borrow money. They are a type of fixed-interest security which is widely used to generate income. They are known as gilt-edged securities or 'gilts' for short. The stock market has given this name to British Government securities because of their reputation as one of the safest investments. The British Government has, over hundreds of years, never failed to meet the interest and capital payments as they fall due.

Relevance for investors

The majority of readers will, I suspect, not be holders of gilts nor attracted to them for a mixture of reasons. Nevertheless they are a major part of the overall UK investment market and many readers will have an indirect interest in gilts through their pension funds, insurance company life funds and because gilts often feature in the investment portfolios of distribution bonds and with-profit bonds. For that reason alone the inclusion of this chapter is relevant and, of course, some readers will hold gilts themselves or may consider doing so in the future.

Range of gilts

The present range of gilts have been issued at different times in the past when the general level of interest rates varied widely.

- They have a variety of maturity dates starting with this year and ending well into the next century.

- They also have different interest rates (known as 'coupons') in relation to their redemption values.

- Because they are guaranteed by the British Government they are attractive to investors, both UK residents and overseas residents, pension funds, trusts etc.

Gilts fall into three main categories when considering investment needs.

- Low coupon – capital growth-orientated stocks.
- High coupon – income-orientated stocks.
- Medium coupon – stocks between the two.

Gilts themselves are divided into five categories.

- Shorts – five years or less to run until redemption.
- Mediums – five to 15 years.
- Longs – over 15 years.
- Undated – no redemption date.
- Index-linked – the return is tied to the movements in the Retail Price Index (RPI).

Those readers who are interested in this area of investment and are possibly thinking about gilts for the first time may at this stage find it useful to have a look at the section on Government Securities in the share price pages in most newspapers, which appears overleaf.

Terminology

Some of the column headings within the table are self-explanatory but some points need further clarification.

Maturity date

The year in the title of the stock is the year when the nominal value is repaid to the holder. Some stocks have two redemption dates, eg '2002–2008', which means that the Government can choose to repay the stock at any time from 2002 onwards but must repay the stock in 2008. It is important to remember that the choice is the Government's, not the investors. The title of the stock contains this vital piece of information and the maturity date is likely to be a major factor in reaching a decision to invest in a particular gilt. The absence of a maturity date, eg 'War Loan 3.5%', means that there is no obligation whatsoever for the Government to redeem all or any of the stock, so income may be paid more or less indefinitely. Clearly this is a very different investment from one which promises full repayment on a pre-

Government Securities

52 week High	Low	Stock	Price	+ or –	Yield Flat	Rm @

Short-dated (up to five years)

52 week High	Low	Stock	Price	+ or –	Yield Flat	Rm @
£104.59	£100.66	Conv 10¼%1999	£100.66	-0.04	9.93	4.85
£104.03	£100.86	Treas 8½% 2000	£100.86	-0.08	–	–
£104.40	£101.42	Conv 9% 2000	£101.42	-0.03	8.77	4.66
£112.22	£105.45	Treas 13% 2000	£105.45	-0.10	12.11	5.04
£105.85	£102.35	Treas 8% 2000	£102.35	-0.10	7.82	5.91
£110.40	£105.13	Treas 10% 2001	£105.13	-0.14	9.52	6.11
£106.49	£101.46	Treas 7% 2001	£101.46	-0.27	6.90	6.25
£108.08	£101.62	Treas 7% 2002	£101.62	-0.32	6.89	6.33
£115.58	£107.16	Exch 9% 2002	£107.16	-0.36	–	–
£117.28	£108.58	Treas 9¼% 2002	£108.58	-0.39	8.98	6.45
£114.74	£105.23	Treas 8% 2003	£105.23	-0.42	7.57	6.24
£123.51	£112.09	Treas 10% 2003	£112.09	-0.51	8.92	6.46
£113.69	£106.24	Treas 13¼% 00-03	£106.24	-0.14	–	–
£110.20	£100.56	Treas 6½% 2003	£100.56	-0.48	6.46	6.34
£114.06	£107.48	Treas 11½% 01-04	£108.32	+0.84	10.72	6.18

Medium-dated (five to fiteeen years)

52 week High	Low	Stock	Price	+ or –	Yield Flat	Rm @
£98.58	£94.90	Treas 5% 2004	£94.90	-0.49	5.08	5.36
£98.00	£91.22	Fndg 3½% 99-04	£91.53	-0.50	3.82	5.54
£126.40	£113.41	Conv 9½%2004	£113.41	-0.85	8.07	5.56
£113.27	£101.89	Treas 6¾% 2004	£101.89	-0.57	6.62	6.31
£125.38	£111.02	Treas 8½% 2005	£111.02	-0.71	7.65	6.31
£128.25	£114.39	Conv 9½% 2005	£114.39	-0.67	8.30	6.37
£135.43	£107.31	Treas 12½% 03-05	£121.77	-0.38	10.01	5.86
£121.64	£107.29	Treas 7½% 06	£107.29	-0.81	6.99	6.22
£122.42	£108.27	Treas 7¾% 06	£108.27	-0.80	7.16	6.25
£111.78	£103.97	Treas 8% 02/06	£103.97	-0.41	7.69	6.51
£126.25	£115.70	Treas 11¾% 03-07	£115.70	-0.36	–	–
£129.86	£113.99	Treas 8½% 2007	£113.99	-0.91	7.46	6.20
£122.55	£107.15	Treas 7½% 2007	£107.15	-0.91	6.76	6.12
£142.63	£127.87	Treas 13½% 04-08	£127.87	-0.46	–	–
£138.52	£120.07	Treas 9% 2008	£120.07	-1.10	7.49	6.07
£132.91	£115.80	Treas 8% 2009	£115.80	-1.69	6.83	5.72
£114.72	£100.05	Treas 5¾% 2009	£100.05	-0.94	5.75	5.74
£118.77	£104.30	Treas 6¼% 2010	£104.30	-0.97	5.99	5.72
£145.30	£127.52	Conv 9% 2011	£127.52	-1.16	7.06	5.75
£147.74	£129.55	Treas 9% 2012	£129.55	-1.20	6.95	5.72
£112.26	£96.39	Treas 5½% 08-12	£96.39	-0.94	5.70	6.02
£139.68	£123.42	Treas 8% 2013	£123.42	-1.23	6.48	5.56
£133.45	£116.80	Treas 7¾% 12-15	£116.80	-1.08	6.63	5.82

Long-dated (over fifteen years)

52 week High	Low	Stock	Price	+ or –	Yield Flat	Rm @
£144.18	£128.58	Treas 8% 2015	£128.58	-1.08	6.22	5.34
£156.12	£140.07	Treas 8¾% 2017	£140.49	-0.94	6.23	5.23
£183.75	£117.50	Exch 12% 13-17	£160.01	-1.58	–	–
£153.27	£136.75	Treas 8% 2021	£138.70	-0.66	5.77	5.04
£131.21	£115.06	Treas 6% 2028	£118.41	-0.37	5.07	4.82

Source: Daily Telegraph 6 October 1999.

Undated

52 week High	Low	Stock	Price	+ or –	Yield Flat	Rm @
£57.00	£46.41	Consols 2½%	£47.94	-0.30	5.21	–
£79.65	£65.53	War Loan 3½%	£68.04	-0.40	5.14	–
£93.25	£74.00	Conversion 3½%	£74.00	-3.50	4.38	–
£174.52	£52.50	Treasury 3%	£53.00	-1.00	5.54	–
£88.15	£72.72	Consols 4%	£74.81	-0.69	5.29	–
£56.00	£45.66	Treasury 2½%	£47.31	-0.29	5.28	–

Indexed Linked on projected inflation of:

52 week High	Low	Stock	Price	+ or –	3%	5%
£206.46	£201.42	Treas 2½% 2001	£202.87	-0.03	3.26	3.82
£207.95	£200.25	Treas 2½% 2003	£201.80	-0.10	2.91	3.21
£134.84	£127.98	Treas 4⅜% 2004	£127.98	-0.16	2.74	2.97
£239.52	£217.44	Treas 2% 2006	£231.84	-0.21	2.01	2.18
£221.38	£197.19	Treas 2½% 2009	£210.98	-0.23	2.15	2.27
£235.76	£206.84	Treas 2½% 2011	£221.46	-0.39	2.26	2.37
£199.14	£172.72	Treas 2½% 2013	£186.03	-0.35	2.26	2.34
£221.31	£189.03	Treas 2½% 2016	£203.51	-2.48	2.20	2.28
£221.81	£185.31	Treas 2½% 2020	£206.22	-0.47	2.13	2.20
£193.87	£157.84	Treas 2½%IL2024	£179.42	-0.46	2.05	2.11
£193.28	£155.66	Treas 4⅛% 2030	£177.60	-0.49	1.99	2.05

@ Yield to Redemption. Source HSBC Bank

10-year Government Bonds

	Yield %	Spread vs Bonds	Spread vs T-Bonds
Belgium	5.40	+0.27	-0.49
Canada	5.72	+0.59	-0.17
France	5.15	+0.02	-0.74
Germany	5.13	–	-0.76
Italy	5.35	+0.22	-0.54
Japan	1.72	-3.41	-4.17
Spain	5.36	+0.23	-0.53
Switzerland	3.25	-1.88	-2.64
Great Britain	5.72	+0.59	-0.17
United States	5.89	+0.76	–

determined date. As a result, undated stocks have not been issued for many years and now have little appeal to investors.

Interest rate (the 'coupon')

All conventional gilts have a fixed rate of interest attached to them known as the 'coupon'. That rate of interest is calculated on the nominal amount of a holding irrespective of the price of the stock in the market. Since prices move all the time and can be above or below par the actual income a new investor receives involves a simple mathematical calculation:

$$\frac{\text{Interest rate x 100}}{\text{Price}} = \text{Yield \%}$$

So, if 12.5% Treasury 2002–05 stands in the market at £125 then a new investor, buying today at that price which is significantly above par, would not receive a return on his investment of 12.5% but would receive:

$$\frac{12.5\% \text{ x } 100}{125} = 10\%$$

Readers will immediately see that once the market price of gilts moves above par or £100 for £100 worth of stock the actual income to a new investor will be less than the coupon rate. If the prices fall below par then the actual return will be in excess of the coupon rate.

At the time writing, with interest rates at a very low level, the prices of nearly all gilts are above par, indeed I could only spot two gilts below par. Looking at 5% Treasury 2004 priced at £97, the initial income to a new investor will be a little in excess of the 5% coupon:

$$\frac{5\% \text{ x } 100}{97} = 5.15\%$$

Flat yield

The result of carrying out the above calculation starting with the 'coupon' produces the initial income to a new investor. That income is known as the 'flat yield'. A careful look at the prices and yields in the press will clearly show that when, as now, most gilts are priced over par, the flat yields will always be less that the coupon rate.

Redemption yields

Because at maturity the British Government repays gilts at par it follows that any bought below par will, at maturity, receive a payout of more than they paid at purchase, ie a capital gain. Similarly, and much more relevant at the present time, is that those buying now at prices above par will be faced with a capital loss at maturity. While that may surprise some readers the fact is that, as with so many investments, it is the overall return that matters.

Redemption yields set out to show a new investor the effect of the known profit or loss spread over the life of the gilt. It may be that figure which prompts the investment to be made initially. Calculating a redemption yield is not difficult. This example shall use 9.5% Conversion 2005 which is priced at £118 with some six-and-a-half years to run to maturity.

The flat yield is
$$\frac{9.5\% \times 100}{118} = 8.05\%$$

Also to be taken into account is the £18 per £100 which will be 'lost' at maturity.

£18 divided over 6.5 years   =   2.76%

So the net redemption yield is   =   5.29%

This is only an approximate method of working out redemption yields, because, for example, the annual 'loss' of £2.76 per £100 is not actually suffered each year but is in reality deducted when the maturity proceeds are paid out in six-and-a-half years time, thus slightly reducing the effect.

Accurate redemption yields on a compound basis can be worked out but only after rather complicated mathematical exercises. In practice they are obtained from bond yield tables.

Index-linked stocks

These are stocks on which both the interest payments and the capital repayment on redemption are adjusted in line with the RPI. Investors are thus protected against the value of their investments being eroded by inflation. However, should the RPI actually fall, then the interest and capital payments are written down.

Index-linked gilts may be attractive to UK taxpayers as any capital gain arising from the inflation adjustment at maturity is not taxed under current legislation. Because capital protection is available, index-linked coupons and yields tend to look much lower than on conventional stocks. What is shown in the papers obviously does not include the value of future inflation protection.

Readers thinking about the merits of index-linked gilts and remembering all that I have written about the effects of inflation upon investment capital, may think that index-linked gilts must be an automatic choice for some investment funds. After all, there is simply no other safe investment opportunity which guarantees inflation-proofing. The main point to make here is that the immediate income is low (currently about 2%) which alone will deter many investors, including those satisfied with modest income levels. While inflation is low and likely to remain low, the benefits of inflation-proofing are also modest.

However, in my view there is a place for index-linked gilts in the portfolios of those investors who are very risk-averse and are willing to accept lower income levels.

What causes gilt prices to change?

A company's share price may change for a number of reasons, namely: because investors alter their views about the earning power of a company; the company releases good or poor performance figures; the company increases dividend payments; or because the shares are perceived to be a 'growth stock'. Gilt prices change because economists and others alter their views about interest rate prospects and also change in response to actual movements in the UK's interest rate structure.

A gilt-edged stock issued at 10% in line with UK interest rates may look unattractive if interest rates increase to 15% causing the price of the stock to fall so that the flat yield approximates current levels. Similarly, if interest rates fall to 6% the market price of the 10% stock will increase dramatically. After all, 10% would be nearly double the 'going rate'.

Readers will now see why the current prices of nearly all gilts are above par. Most were issued some years ago when interest rates in the UK were higher than they are now.

Are gilts a good investment?

Traditionally, most smaller investors have steered clear of gilts due to the perceived complexities, coupled with the fact that they have to be bought through a stockbroker and are subject to the usual dealing costs as set out in Appendix 9. In addition, banks and building societies have captured the public savings habit so well that gilts have been the preserve of the more knowledgeable/wealthier investor.

There can be no doubt at all that when interest rates are historically very high, investments in gilts can generally offer the prospect of capital gains when interest rates drop. Indeed, the proof of that is in the prices of most gilts today where some holdings are at prices of up to £130. Some holders of those stocks, probably bought for income, are now seeing generous capital gains. It should also be made very clear at this point that should interest rates rise in the UK, that would lead to an overall reduction in the prices of gilts.

It seems that at the present time few investors will feel inclined to rush into buying gilts for themselves. However, the position may change. Gilts are still a sensible investment for some trusts and charities as part of a balanced portfolio.

Buying and selling gilt-edged stocks

There is a very active market in gilts and there are two ways for the private investor to access this market:

1. through a stockbroker or bank;
2. using the brokerage service provided by the Bank of England.

Using a stockbroker or bank is relatively simple. Both will accept instructions to buy or sell either nominal sums, eg £5,000 of 6.5% Treasury Stock 2003 or to invest the sum of £5,000 in the same stock. A guide to stockbrokers' usual charges is included in Appendix 9.

The Bank of England provides a 'Brokerage Service' as an alternative way for the private investor to buy and sell gilts by post. This facility was previously known as the 'National Savings Register'. The commission charges are generally much lower than the charges made for buying or selling through a stockbroker or a bank. Gilts may be bought or sold this way by completing the relevant form which is available from post offices or by telephoning the Bank of England on Freephone 0800–818–614.

The Bank of England issues a publication *Investing in Gilts – A Private Investor's Guide* which is available at no charge and which provides further information on all aspects in investing in Government stocks.

The taxation of gilts

The taxation treatment is straightforward. As from April 1998 all interest paid on gilts is paid gross, ie no income tax is deducted at source. That can be particularly useful for non-taxpayers who would like to receive their interest gross rather than net and have to reclaim some income tax annually. However, all such interest is assessable to tax and should be included on any income tax return submitted. Any profits which arise when gilts mature are free of CGT as are any profits earned if gilts are sold in the market prior to maturity. The inflation uplift component of the capital amount of index-linked gilts is therefore also tax free. Not surprisingly, any losses incurred do not qualify for relief from CGT. The Inland Revenue explanatory leaflet IR69 gives guidance on the tax treatment of accrued interest.

Any readers who held gilts prior to April 1998 and who are receiving the half-yearly interest payment with income tax deducted at the savings rate of 20%, and who would like to receive that interest gross, should obtain the relevant application form from the Bank of England. Each form can be used for holdings of different stocks.

16 Guaranteed Investment Products

Stock market volatility along with low interest rates has lead to a general increase in the issue of guaranteed equity products. Although inflation has been reduced to historically low levels, and seems likely to remain low, it is still a problem for the long-term investor. For risk-averse investors the prospect of being able to obtain some capital growth coupled with protection against the downside can look attractive.

The range of guaranteed investments stretches from a simple six months', fixed-interest savings account to guaranteed rolling funds and fixed-term income or capital growth bonds. Some offer multiple levels of guarantee which can be determined at the beginning of each quarter, plus exposure to all the major markets' indices.

However, guaranteed investment should itself be approached with caution. It is very easy to place too much reliance on the word 'guarantee' and believe that it means simply 'no loss whatsover', whereas that may not be the whole story.

Categories of product

Guaranteed investment is split into two main categories of products which differ substantially in structure.

Guaranteed life products

Guaranteed life products provide capital growth or an income through the use of endowment policies and the favourable treatment of tax. These generally are for fixed terms of between one and five years. There is usually a minimum initial investment of £3,000. Income is always paid net of savings-rate tax but higher-rate taxpayers will have a liability of 17%. There is no liability to capital gains tax. These products therefore are rarely attractive to higher-rate taxpayers.

Guaranteed equity products

Guaranteed equity products are the main topic of this chapter. These products fall into two broad types: quarterly rolling funds which are an on-going investment and which can be accessed at any time; and fixed-period bonds which generally run for between one and five years. Most of these bonds are structured around derivatives – an explanatory note is included in Appendix 11.

There are never many of these products available to investors because their appeal is limited. At the time of writing there are just ten investment houses marketing them, although some products are available with differing levels of guarantee (see later).

All these guaranteed or protected funds promise to shelter investors from the worst stock market downturns. If markets fall steeply, investors' losses will be restricted to a small percentage of the real fall. If markets rise then investors are promised a share of the growth too.

Here we have to distinguish between products which offer a 100% guarantee of no loss (less a possible initial 5%), and those where investors can select a level of protection usually between 95% and 100% of their initial sum. The latter type is generally referred to as a 'protected investment'.

The important difference for readers to grasp is that the higher the level of guarantee, the less will b the share of any stock market growth. Specific examples are outlined below.

Close Brothers Escalator Fund

This is a quarterly rolling fund which has no investment term and offers levels of protection between 100% to 90%. There is no limitation on upward growth subject to the level of protection chosen.

Allied Dunbar's Guaranteed Equity Bond

Offers no loss if the FTSE 100 falls, but upward growth is limited to between 20% and 40% of the FTSE 100 growth.

So one product offers maximum protection with restricted growth, the other a low level of risk coupled with increased scope for capital growth. In both products, gains are locked in over a pre-determined period, usually three months. Some of these products can pay out income but more often there is simply no income option – all of the income generated is added to the fund.

That may be acceptable but investors need to be certain about this from the outset.

Matters to consider

Readers will now see why these products deserve an inclusion in *The Bad Investment Guide*. The exact nature of any product offered by an adviser or being considered by an investor needs to be very carefully assessed. Investors should pause and not be overly impressed by the use of the word 'guarantee' which can have very comforting connotations. In particular, investors should consider the following.

1. What exactly is being guaranteed here, income or capital? There is a world of difference between a National Savings Guaranteed Income Bond and the equity-protected products dealt with in this chapter. The guarantes applied to no-risk income products are covered elsewhere in this book.

2. If one is considering an equity-guaranteed product without any income withdrawal facility, is that really acceptable over the longer period?

3. Given that the protection costs money, the protected investor therefore receives poorer returns than the unprotected investor should the market rise. The cost of that protection lasts over the whole life of the investment; it is not phased out in some way after a period or time or if the investment has significantly increased in value.

4. There is a strong argument that guaranteed equity or protected products act as an unnecessary shackle on stock market growth as over the long term any falls in the market will be ironed out by subsequent growth, rendering the guarantee worthless.

As an adviser I was never very keen on guaranteed products for some of the above reasons, but I do accept that there will be some for whom they appeal. It can sometimes be a useful exercise to look at one portfolio and then ask oneself the following question: 'How will my investment perform in time of high growth, low growth or a stock market setback?' If one is heavily biased in favour of low-risk investments then these guaranteed products may have no place. On the other hand, if one is heavily exposed to higher-risk investments, or one has no exposure whatsoever to equity investments, they may have a place.

Performance

At this stage it may be worthwhile to pause and look at how these guaranteed equity funds have performed over one year to June 1999 when total returns from the FTSE 100 were 9.68%.

Fund	% Change over 1 Year
Family Safety Net Stockmarket	2.73
Close UK Escalator 100	−0.14
Govet UK Equity Safeguard	−0.75
Edinburgh Safety First	−1.00
Close World Escalator	−1.49
Close US Escalator	−1.88
Govett UK Safeguard	−1.93
Morgan Grenfell All Weather	−2.00
Close UK Escalator 95	−2.06
Scottish Widows UK Sheltered Growth	−2.30
Govett US Equity Safeguard	−3.10
NatWest Safeguard	−3.33
Lloyds TSB Safety First	−7.91

Source: Micropal. June 1999.

Readers may ask themselves why these funds are losing money in a rising market and why there are such enormous differences between the funds. The answer lies in how and when the protection is bought, how guarantees are constructed, how funds are managed and how much is levied in charges. Investors in the top few may feel inclined to accept the result philosophically, but investors in the bottom few could feel let down by their investment managers.

The *Investors Chronicle* for 11 June 1999 carried the above figures below the headline 'Abysmal Showing by Guaranteed Funds'. The figures seem fair enough but they are of course just a photograph at one moment in time. Had there been a major stock market setback then the headline would have been very different and investors would have thought 'thank goodness for protection'.

In 1993 as a practising IFA, I had the job of investing some £100,000 for a higher-rate taxpayer aged 63 who wanted low-risk capital growth and was still smarting over poor investment advice received elsewhere in the past. He had no need of income as he had generous pensions.

At the time, and for that amount, it seemed sensible to place some funds in overseas markets, mainly Europe and the Far East, but all investment gurus were predicting a dramatic rise in the Japanese stock market. I was influenced by that argument and with reservation placed £10,000 in Japanese equities but via an AIG Life (UK) protected fund. In 1995 the Japanese stock market collapsed on the back of the Kobe earthquake and both the client and I were hugely grateful for the safety net of the AIG Life (UK) fund. Subsequently the Nikkei recovered. Four years later, at the time of writing the guarantee has been activated and that investment is worth £10,004! That is somewhat disappointing, bearing in mind that the same money in an average UK growth fund would have nearly doubled. However, had that investment not had the guarantee built in, it would now be worth about £8,560 which points to an overall loss of 14% or about 3.5% pa. The guarantee achieved considerable peace of mind for both adviser and client and avoided an unwelcome loss. The investment, together with others made in Japan at that time, may increase in value and go on to deliver a good investment return, but that seems to be a long way off yet. In the meantime, should that investor get tired of waiting or require his funds, the benefit of the guarantee is self-evident.

Conclusion

Readers, as always, will have to decide for themselves. I remain unenthusiastic about guaranteed/protected products but remember that they can be used alongside their unprotected counterparts thus offering a more balanced investment portfolio as the above example illustrates.

For investors seeking to reduce or to limit investment risk that aim can be achieved by using lower risk products such as with-profit bonds, distribution bonds, UK Equity & Bond unit trusts, cautious managed life funds and ZDPs instead of protected products.

17 Ethical Investments

Ethical issues are changing our lives – the way we work, what we buy, how we travel, what we eat. Some think that we are experiencing an ethical explosion. From an investor's point of view there in undoubtedly an increased awareness of ethical investment criteria which has resulted in sales of relevant products. According to the Ethical Investment Research and Information Service (EIRIS), as at June 1999 the money invested in ethical funds exceeded £2.5 billion on behalf of 300,000 unit and policyholders. As a result of this increased awareness, many financial advisers now incorporate an appropriate question to raise with new clients. I followed that practice as an IFA.

What is an ethical investment? Arriving at an exact definition is tricky, but broadly speaking it is where ethical considerations influence the choice of investments. A recent survey by EIRIS showed that more than 70% of adults questioned would be influenced by ethical considerations if given a choice of where their money was to be invested. My experience as an IFA is that few investors take that view, and, if they do, choice is often limited to the avoidance of alcohol and tobacco-related companies.

There are currently more than 30 providers offering over 40 ethical funds, comprising unit trusts, investment trusts, ISAs, pensions, FSAVCs, mortgage repayment options and life insurance products. Generally, ethical investment means avoiding investing in companies that generate significant business profits from:

- alcohol or tobacco
- export of goods or services for military use
- supplying ozone-depleting chemicals
- testing cosmetics or toiletries on animals
- using intensive farming methods
- extraction/importation of tropical hardwood
- trading in prohibited pesticides
- activities which pollute waterways
- companies which have registered subsidiaries in a significant number of countries identified as violating human rights

Ethical funds vary in their screening techniques, by the sophistication of their ethical 'thinking' and the extent to which they lobby companies to become more ethical. Some companies, although operating in one or more of the areas listed above, do issue policy statements claiming that they operate on a 'green' policy basis, ie they take positive steps not to endanger the enviroment by:

- careful handling of waste material
- conserving energy
- avoiding harmful emissions
- reducing noise nuisance
- disposing of containers responsibly

Further positive criteria, which may appeal to investors, are claims that a company will adopt certain criteria in its overall management policies such as:

- community involvement
- equal opportunities
- trade union and employee participation
- the provision of training

Running contrary to the above is the view that no public limited company can possibly meet the highest ethical standards because to some extent they all indulge in unethical practices, or a subsidiary produces goods that contribute to unethical activities. The banking sector is a good example. All UK banks clearly do not damage the environment or pollute, but they do finance brewers, chemical companies and farms. Precision engineering companies may manufacture lathes or other capital goods that are then used to manufacture bullets; mining companies or chemical companies may produce chemicals used in pesticides.

The problem for investors and their advisers includes the hidden cost of operating ethically. If investors wish ethical considerations to be taken into account, the amount of emphasis to be given in formulating investment plans needs to be determined. The fact that some investment opportunities are excluded may affect overall investment performance.

Ultimately it all depends upon the degree to which an investor wishes ethical issues to influence investment decisions.

Effect upon investment performance

For some years there was evidence that ethical investment did not necessarily impede the overall performance of ethical unit trusts and adopting ethical policies therefore should have little impact on total returns. However, it does now seem that there is evidence to the contrary, and those seeking to include ethical considerations in their investment choices are likely to sustain a reduction in overall performance.

How ethical funds fared over 1 year and 5 years to June 1999

Fund	£1,000 over 5 yrs	Rank	£1,000 over 1 yr	Rank	Fund size £m
Credit Suisse Fellowship	1923	1	948	13	100.7
Sovereign Ethical	1814	2	960	11	22.6
TSB Enviromental Inv	1803	3	1094	3	25.5
Framlington Health	1765	4	728	19	66.0
Friends Stewardship	1746	5	1022	6	530.8
CIS Enviromental	1669	6	980	10	151.4
Scot Equitable Ethical	1654	7	958	12	44.0
Jupiter Ecology	1648	8	932	14	68.6
Allchurches Amity	1613	9	984	9	36.8
Aberdeen Ethical	1490	10	925	15	7.2
Equitable Ethical	1449	11	993	8	21.4
Abbey Ethical	1384	12	897	16	43.5
Friends Stewardship Inc	1358	13	1006	7	75.3
City Financial Acorn Ethical	1357	14	876	17	4.1
Clerical medical Evergreen	1090	15	825	18	18.5
Henderson Ethical	n/a		1034	5	40.8
FPAM Ins Ex Ethical UK Eq	n/a		1070	4	86.4
Friends Stewardship Int	n/a		1099	1	29.5
NPI Global Care Income	n/a		1096	2	£33.7
Ethical average	1523		958		
Average for all unit trusts	1732		1114		
FT All Share Index	2241		1112		
Average of the four unit trust sectors in which these trusts appear	1890		1048		

Figures are calculated on an offer to bid basis with net income reinvested.
Source: Micropal. June 1999.

Ethical considerations for an investor buying individual shares

The previous pages set out some of the main points regarding ethical investment. Provided that an investor, who wishes to apply ethical considerations to their investment decisions, is prepared to use collective investment schemes of some kind, they can rely on fund managers to carry out vetting processes on their behalf. Such an investor can study the criteria behind various schemes and pick managers who nearest match their views on this topic. Alternatively, of course, an investor could be less fussy and instead pick a good performing fund out of those included in the table above.

However, investors who buy individual shares and who wish to adopt an ethical approach, are faced with a dilemma in implementing such a policy. It would be relatively easy, for example, to exclude tobacco and brewery companies, but applying the other wider criteria would prove difficult for the average private investor.

One way forward might be to obtain a copy of the latest published accounts. Nowadays these often include an 'Environmental Report' or some other similar statement of the company's practice which might be sufficient to satisfy some investors. At the time of writing, I noticed such inclusions in the annual accounts for 'Shell' Transport and Trading Co plc and Royal & Sun Alliance plc.

A better way forward may be to use the services of EIRIS' information and research facilities. Depending upon an investor's ethical stance they can provide details of which companies an investor would wish to support and the ones to avoid. EIRIS researches more than 1,200 UK company groups and produces fact-sheets. They also produce a bi-monthly newsletter the *Ethical Investor* which covers a wide range of issues relating to ethical investment.

It is outside the scope of this book to cover all aspects of ethical investment. The point of the inclusion of this chapter in *The Bad Investment Guide* is to help and guide readers and to provide basis knowledge on the matter.

Readers seeking more information should contact:

Ethical Investment Research and Information Service
80–84 Bondway
London SW8 1SF
Tel: 020-7840–5700

18 Investing in Property

Until the development of stock markets, property was virtually the only reasonably dependable asset-backed investment. The rental income from an agricultural or commercial property is to some extent a substitute for a dividend from the business that occupies the property. The following are features of property investment in the past which still apply to some extent today.

- If business thrives substantially because of the location or the quality of the land, demand for property rises and with it rents and land values.

- Property values only follow business profitability in very general terms and the property cycle is likely to be different from the business cycle.

- Tenants have to pay their rent even when they make a loss, so property has some of the characteristics of fixed-interest securities.

- If property becomes vacant and tenants cannot be found or there is delay then there can be a serious loss of income.

- Property owners have legal rights and obligations that substantially affect the value of their investments.

- There are special issues such as planning policy, which can greatly affect property values.

- The commercial and residential property markets are very different and may move in different directions.

Property investment is an asset-backed investment and can therefore provide long-term protection against inflation. Property has several characteristics which make it very different from equities and is certainly an option for diversification when a broad range of equity-related investments is already held.

This chapter sets out the broad considerations and some of the advantages and disadvantages of property investment, which will only appeal to a very small number of investors. In addition, no effort has been made to try to cover all the income tax and CGT considerations which apply.

With low inflation and interest rates at a 30-year low (and both likely to remain so) some investors are seriously considering buying property. Indeed, there is anecdotal evidence of some astute, younger (and maybe wealthier) people buying a second property, helped by a second mortgage, to rent out instead of, or as well as, making payments into a pension plan (see later under 'Residential property and pension planning').

Property, as an investment, can offer:

- immediate income;
- the prospect of an increasing income;
- the prospect of capital growth.

General advantages of property investment

1. Historically, property has kept its value. It has often been claimed that property never falls in value, but the last recession of 1989–1992 clearly proved that to be very wrong.

2. A reasonable certainty of income, coupled with rent reviews which should ensure that the rent can be moved upwards in line with inflation or with a general increase in rentals to keep pace with rental values for similar properties in the area.

3. Possibly a measure of capital growth. Statistically, taken over the long term and taken very generally, property values have outstripped inflation, and therefore provided a hedge against inflation (with the hope of doing better).

4. Some investors just prefer the tangible nature of property, possibly linked to familiarity.

5. Reasonably favourable treatment for income tax purposes.

General disadvantages of property investment

1. Property is relatively expensive to buy and to sell. Legal fees, stamp duty and agents fees all mount up.

2. Property often takes time to sell, even in a good market. The time between obtaining vacant possession and receiving the cash can take months.

3. Unlike listed securities it is usually not possible to sell properties in bits to boost income or re-arrange investments generally or take advantage of the annual CGT allowance.

4. Letting property is a bit like running a business. It requires all the administrative, financial and marketing skills that are needed in most enterprises, and also involves commitment and patience in dealing with tenants. Some of these disadvantages can be overcome, or at least reduced, through the use of a management agency, although that will mean a reduction in income.

Quantifying the investment risk

1. Poor tenants who do not pay the rent or misuse the property.
2. Loss of income due to periods of non-occupation (voids).
3. The on-going cost of repairs and maintenance.
4. The absence of capital growth – this can be a major adverse factor.

Readers considering property investment will, I suspect, be only interested in considering lower-priced properties which would have the following uses:

- student lettings;
- shorthold domestic lettings;
- holiday flats;
- mixed properties, ie shops with flats above;
- buying to rent for the longer term (referred to later).

As a result the remainder of this chapter will consider the above circumstances only and not cover the market in much larger and more expensive commercial properties at prices of £500,000 and above. The factors surrounding those investment properties are very different from the areas under consideration to the average personal investor.

Various initial assessments to be made by a prospective investor

1. Do I know enough about the property market in a particular area to be able to assess the risks and rewards? If not possibly seek professional help.

2. Am I making an investment as such or am I really taking on running a small business? If the latter is the case, is the time and commitment available?

3. Is the initial income (the 'return') attractive and does is compensate for the disadvantages? How does it compare with the immediate returns available of deposit-based or other asset-backed investments?

4. What are the chances of obtaining capital growth?

We have all heard stories of stunningly successful property investments (the owners of such are often only too pleased to talk about them). Only rarely does one hear about poor or sometime disastrous property adventures (such owners are understandably reluctant to talk about such setbacks). At the time of writing, there are streets of boarded-up terraced houses in parts of Manchester and other towns in the North of England which have little or no value – some owner-occupiers will have lost out very badly, as will many people who have bought there for investment purposes. The change in shopping habits in favour of out-of-town supermarkets has affected the selling prices of shops. Indeed, there are many high streets with numerous empty shops which, a few years ago, would have sold readily but now stand empty with little chance of attracting new tenants. If prospective tenants are interested the rents are bound to be low and, whilst empty, mean a significant loss of income for somebody.

Do I know enough about the property market?

Where a property is situated is always said to be the most important issue affecting its value. Very small differences in location, from one street to another, can make substantial differences to values and prospects for growth. Some areas are 'improving', some are 'static' and others are 'depreciating'. Often it is possible to see the reasons which can be self-evident, such as the decline in local industry or closure of a major employer.

Assessing an area for student lettings may be a different exercise from an assessment for holiday lettings. Some parts of the South East have benefited enormously from the prosperity attached to newer industries and that benefit has totally by-passed much of the North. The building of the M25 was believed to trigger an increase in the price of some properties. The precision required to assess an area will depend upon the type of property one wants to invest in, which will include the present demand/supply for student lettings or holiday flats or which form of property investment is favoured. Prospective investors should make their own enquiries from estate agents and property management companies and by checking on the range of properties for sale.

Another way to approach the matter is to try to assess what types of property are likely to be successful in any area. If there is a shortage of flats or smaller properties available to rent, then rents will be higher and more attractive to the investor than if the opposite is the case. It may be a matter or trying to get close to the likely market by reading the local press and talking to estate agents.

Am I making an investment or running a small business?

The main disadvantage of all property investment must be the time, skills and efforts needed to manage them. As mentioned above, that can be reduced by the use of a management company or letting agents. Agency fees vary greatly. Some charge on the basis of 10%–15% of the rents collected. Others charge a fee for each letting, plus a collection fee. A useful method of trying to avoid taking on undesirable new tenants is to use an agency just to obtain and vet a new tenant. For that service some agencies charge one months' rent. Thereafter, the owner assumes full control and responsibility. Some larger properties rented to students are simply not attractive to a management company so any owner must be prepared to handle the day-to-day management themselves. A word of caution is needed with regard to the appointment of managing agents. Anyone can set up as a letting agent without qualifications, experience or indeed money. If you decide to use an agent pick one who is a member of an association with a published code of conduct.

There are some people who like the idea of running a rented property themselves and for them the management problems simply do not exist. The success of the venture will then depend upon devoting the time and efforts needed. Other skills needed include the following:

- Obtaining and vetting new tenants and avoiding 'bad payers'.
- Dealing with difficult tenants and slow payers.
- Meeting the requirements of a local authority or university if either body is involved in placing tenants.
- Meeting the statutory payments for council tax, water charges etc.
- Day-to-day repairs and maintenance.
- Coping with changes in legislation, ie annual gas inspections and the soft furniture fire regulations.
- Being aware of the implications of the Housing Act 1996 which impose

special obligations on landlords in respect of Houses in Multiple Occupation (HMOs). That obligation is to register the property with the local authority. The implication of this requirement is not set out in full here. Any readers considering this type of property investment should approach their local authority for a copy of their guidance notes.

Is the property investment attractive financially?

Most property investment will produce an initial income. The first test is to compare the return on the investment with the yield on alternatives such as shares or gilts.

$$\text{Initial yield} = \frac{\text{Annual rental income x 100}}{\text{Price of property}}$$

The price of the property will be the initial investment, including acquisition costs, improvements, furnishings etc – the total outlay needed to generate the income. That percentage should reflect the work and the risk. So with a house let to students one might expect to receive a return of 15%–17%, but a house let to a family on a shorthold lease would be less at around 8%. Holiday flats will probably earn a high return during the summer but minimal amounts (if empty or let at a low rent) in the winter – it is the overall average that applies.

At this stage it is necessary to be aware of the average rates offered on deposit-based and asset-backed investments. Generally for the types of property under discussion here the return should be higher. In the cases of properties calling for a high level of management the returns should be considerably higher.

At the time of writing these returns are approximately:

- Building society higher rates   5% – 6.5% gross
- Corporate Bond funds   6% – 7% gross
- Average return of FTSE stocks   2.30% net
- Higher-income bond   9% net – 11.25% gross

The returns available in my area of Lancashire are approximately:

- For student houses   Up to 16% gross
- For shorthold leases   7% – 11% gross
- For holiday flats   Possibly 15%
- For mixed commercial properties, shops etc   12%

The prospects for capital growth

This may be a major factor when considering any property investment. However, in times of low interest rates the annual income generated may become more important to the investor. In the UK, residential property prices are driven by the owner-occupier market in contrast with other parts of Europe. In the long term, residential property prices tend to follow earnings growth. In general the ratio of prices to earnings has been about 3:1.

There can be variations in this trend, such as the late 1980s where property prices rose so high that that ratio reached 4.6:1. The residential property market collapsed in 1989 when prices fell with the economic recession and the phenomena and misery of 'negative equity' appeared.

However, I suspect that the majority of those considering a property investment are motivated by either a wish to own property and run it as a business to increase their income, or to aim for above-average capital growth. Taking the latter point, it does seem that the key to buying a relatively cheap property with the aim of capital growth depends upon identifying an area which is going to improve. It can be a good approach to seek out an area with a large transient population and big employers. Employers whose general business is growing will be an additional positive feature.

There are more and less desirable areas in nearly every town. Look to see if there is a dearth of family homes to rent and if so a house rather than a flat would be prudent. Student lettings call for a location near to the college and if not, certainly one on a good bus route.

The prospect for capital growth on shop properties, and shops with flats above, would appear to be very suspect at the present time and so great care is needed. However 'cheap' such a property may seem, unless someone can run a viable retail business from the site there will be few interested in renting. We are said to be a nation of shopkeepers but that description is changing, so, if it proves difficult to obtain a tenant for a shop, then:

- the initial rent is bound to be low;
- there is a likelihood of periods of non-occupation;
- tenants may struggle to meet the rent or cease business;
- the chance of capital growth will be non-existent.

Prime locations probably remain sound property investments, provided that an area does not deteriorate or suffer from a major retail development nearby. However, out-of-town shops are probably best avoided.

The overall past performance of property is quite hard to assess due to the wide differences in parts of the UK and the range of investment properties. London and the South East have been special cases. Some years ago property prices in Aberdeen shot up on the back of North Sea oil. More recently rental prices in Edinburgh escalated in anticipation of the Scottish Assembly. Property agents are currently favouring Cambridge, Oxford, Leeds and parts of Manchester as good investment areas.

Overall, property has not been nearly as good over the last 15 years as equity-related investments as the following performance figures make clear.

Property investment performance

It is not easy to provide a helpful comparison of the long-term differences in investment performance between property and the alternatives. This is due, in part at least, to the very wide differences in capital growth between different parts of the UK and also the wide differences in the rental income and capital growth of different types of property.

The best, and rather crude, measures that I have been able to locate are:

Returns v volatility

	1974–1997	
	Return	Volatility
Residential property	14%	11%
Equities	18%	34%
Gilts	13%	16%
Building Society 90 days' notice	10%	Nil

Source: *Money Management.* August 1999.

Volatility is a measure of investment returns against a standard deviation. In general terms, lower volatility points to lower risks and may make any investment more attractive than one with higher volatility. Increased volatility needs to be viewed against other investment returns or total returns.

Readers who wish to investigate this further could approach organisations that maintain statistics, including Halifax plc, Nationwide Building Society, Jones Lang La Salle and the Valuation Office Agency (previously part of the Inland Revenue).

Residential property and pension planning

Residential property is not available as an investment through either a SIPP or a SASS. In both cases only commercial property is permitted. However, could residential property be considered as a general alternative to a conventional pension plan? It is now possible to borrow up to 80% against the purchase price of a property, which is then let. Fixed rates are also available. In many cases the rental income will cover the costs of running the property, including meeting the interest and capital repayments on the loan. The objective is for the loan to be fully repaid in 20 or 25 years when the property will have appreciated in value, the rental value will have increased, and an income provided for the investor in lieu of a pension. Using the growth rates quoted above (namely 18% for equities and 14% for residential properties), and assuming that an initial lump sum of £20,000 was available from a 40% taxpayer, future projections. show that the pension route was far superior and delivered a far greater return over 25 years. The residential property investment did well and delivered a return of nearly 11% net of tax but, of course, the loan has to be repaid and there is the possibility of a liability to CGT on sale which would be a disadvantage compared with the pension plan which allows for 25% of the fund to be withdrawn free of tax.

For the purposes of *The Bad Investment Guide* it seems that residential property may not stand up as a genuine alternative to proper pension planning. However, it may be worth considering in the following circumstances as a way of providing:

- a pension for an individual (such as a non-working spouse) with no relevant earnings and hence no ability to build a pension;

- an additional pension for an individual close to retirement, with inadequate pension provisions. This may apply to a high earner who can possibly set some income aside to boost loan repayments to ensure that a loan is cleared over a short period.

Buying to rent

The increase in property prices in 1998 and 1999, coupled with low interest rates and the sudden willingness of lenders to provide 'buy to rent' mortgages, has led to a sudden increase in investors' enthusiasm for buying to rent. This trend has fuelled price increases in some areas and has even lead to an over-supply of properties to rent. This has resulted in a continuous rise in property prices coupled with a reduction in rentals, thereby reducing the attractiveness of these investments. The moral is clear – those interested need to do their homework very carefully.

One big attraction of buying to rent is that it offers the ability to gear-up. Suppose that an investor has £50,000 available for a property investment. Instead of buying for around £50,000 the investor takes out a mortgage of £50,000 and buys a property for £100,000. The additional rental income generated will more than cover the interest and loan repayments on the £50,000 borrowed, so spendable income should not suffer. However, if the property increases in value the investor stands to double that increase in value. This investor could borrow more, possibly up to £250,000, as the initial £50,000 will provide a 20% deposit. However, an investor has to ensure that they can handle a property investment of that size and meet the capital repayments on the loan and that their overall finances can cope with an increase in interest rates, unless they are able to borrow on fixed terms.

A survey produced in 1999 by the University of York showed that private rents had risen by 2.3% over the previous year compared with an increase of 4.4% in house prices, thus reducing profitability to new landlords.

All the evidence at the time of writing is that buying to let is not a short-term, quick-return investment and that investors should view it on a medium term of around ten years. That is not to say that some won't get lucky and be able to sell on with sitting tenants or with vacant possession in a year or two!

The need for help from a solicitor

I am sure that all readers will be aware of the dangers to landlords in letting out any property without making certain that the legal basis of the rental agreement is as sound as possible from the landlord's point of view. This applies to all forms of letting, including students (who you would fully expect to leave at the end of the academic year). It is outside the scope of this book to try to cover all the aspects of this complicated area. Instead it is mentioned to highlight a matter which requires considerable care and help from your solicitor.

Conclusion

Direct investment in commercial property is impossible for the smaller investor and can present serious problems of diversification for even the richest individuals. However, a number of indirect investment vehicles are available for property investment including:

- shares in listed property companies;
- insurance company property funds;
- property unit trusts.

Readers will be able to refer back to comments on these investment schemes, together with pointers for assessing past performance and initial yields.

The overriding factors which govern a decision to make a direct property investment will probably be emotional ones, namely to actually own the bricks and mortar, coupled with a belief in its 'value' and possibly a desire to run it as a small business.

19 Investing Offshore

Introduction

Offshore funds are broadly those funds established outside the UK – normally in low tax areas. Offshore funds have become of greater importance in recent years as more and more UK investment managers and insurance companies have established and promoted offshore-based products. In addition the European Union (EU) has encouraged the promotion of cross-border financial services and this has contributed to the increased awareness of this area of investment. The abolition of PEPs and TESSAs may have added to this trend.

Overview

Offshore funds, particularly those based in the Channel Islands and the Isle of Man, have a long history in the UK where they have been available to UK resident and domiciled investors, to UK expatriates and non-UK domiciled individuals working in this country.

In recent years, because of increased investor awareness, offshore funds have been established in the EU tax havens of Dublin and Luxembourg.

The financial services industry has contributed to the degree of mythology about the benefits of offshore investment and, indeed, has actively promoted the concept of 'tax-free roll-up'. For an individual who is a UK resident and is UK domiciled there are no tax benefits other than the payment of income gross and possible tax deferral. In many instances there will be a definite tax disadvantage, especially if the selected offshore fund itself invests in UK shares. The picture changes for UK expatriates who are classed as non-residents for tax purposes, non-UK domiciled UK resident investors and some foreigners who wish to invest in the UK and who can be certain that such investments fit comfortably with their own tax regimes.

For some there may be both income tax and CGT advantages and, possibly, inheritance tax benefits.

The relevance to readers of *The Bad Investment Guide*

Although the appeal of offshore investments has broadened from a minority to a much wider range of investors, it is still likely to remain the preserve of relatively wealthy and perhaps more sophisticated investors. This chapter is included to offer some advice and guidance to any readers holding offshore investments, or those who may have offshore products recommended to them by financial advisers. It is appropriate to make clear here that this chapter does not try to cover the merits or risks for UK investors who have direct holdings in overseas stocks and shares; that is a separate topic.

It seems most likely that readers will be UK resident and domiciled and therefore liable to UK taxes. This chapter is written principally with this in mind. For those other readers who fall outside those parameters, although this chapter may help, they probably require more detailed information to reflect their personal financial circumstances.

The terminology of offshore investments

SICAVs

The most common type of investment fund in Europe is the Société d'Investissement à Capital Variable or SICAV. This type of investment company with variable capital is the model for the UK open-ended investment company. The investment is expressed in shares rather than units and more shares are created as required. It is very similar to a UK unit trust.

UCITS

Undertakings for Collective Investments in Transferable Securities (UCITS) is not another form of investment, but instead is a fund which has been issued with a certificate stating that it complies with the EU UCITS Directive.

OEICs

Open-Ended Investment Companies (OEICs) are the UK equivalent of SICAVs.

Umbrella funds

The OEICs structure allows many management groups to offer 'umbrella funds'. These give the investor a choice of funds covering a range of investment areas, each sector being a different class of share within the one company. Switches between funds therefore become a simple matter of share exchange, often at no cost.

FSA-recognised or non-FSA authorised

The former are authorised for sale in the UK under the terms of the Financial Services Act 1986 and satisfy Department of Trade and Industry requirements on regulation and investor protection. The latter are regulated in their home country.

Products available offshore

There is a wide range of offshore products available. In the main they are dominated by savings and investments. Almost all products are variations of the investment bond which of course offers:

- almost tax-free roll-up (see below);
- an option to withdraw up to 5% of the initial investment as income and those withdrawals are 'tax free' in the hands of the investor;
- for UK residents no tax to pay until full or partial encashment.

In addition, there are pension products, protection products, long-term care and estate-planning products available. Some of these products carry names which are pointers to their specialised investment objective. One of the more controversial types of offshore investment in recent years has been the personalised offshore bond. This contract allows direct investment into equities, stocks, currencies, fixed interest securities and bonds – in fact anything that is required. No matter what the underlying investments are, the bond still enjoys all the advantages listed above plus a possible further advantage in that whereas each underlying investment, if held separately, would need separate recording and entry on tax forms, once held inside such a bond only one type of income is received and, furthermore, that may not need to be included on a tax return. The downside is that the charges can be quite high and there may also be charges levied on the underlying investments.

Investor protection

Investor protection schemes in the Channel Islands and the Isle of Man are at least as good and in many respects superior to those provided in the UK. Luxembourg and Dublin are also well regulated. As an IFA, I felt quite comfortable recommending products based in those centres. However, it is unlikely that I would have recommended a collective scheme located outside those areas. I still feel the same way now and apply that to my own investments.

Taxation treatment of funds

The term 'gross roll-up' has often been used to describe these funds and was very often the basis on which they were promoted. It is a misnomer, which is best prefaced by the word 'almost'. Although offshore funds are based in tax havens and pay very little or no tax directly, they are not completely free of tax. If an offshore fund invests directly in equities, the dividends it receives will normally be subject to non-reclaimable withholding tax. This is a minor inconvenience in low-yielding markets such as Japan, but is a more significant loss in higher-yielding markets, like the UK.

Investments in fixed-interest securities will probably be tax free. However, the fund itself may have to pay a small amount of tax directly. For example, Jersey funds are subject to a small, flat, corporation tax charge. In Luxembourg the rate is between 0.03% and 0.06%.

Tax payable by the investor

The individual tax position of each fund will depend upon which type of fund is chosen – distributor or non-distributor. Distributor funds are SICAVs, OEICs or UCITS, which distribute at least 85% of their income each year.

For most UK investors, distribution funds are to be preferred. Any dividends paid are regarded as gross income. Any capital gains arising on the sale of shares in the fund are subject to the normal CGT treatment.

A non-distributor fund is any fund which has not been categorised as a distributor fund by the Inland Revenue. This is the case even if the fund would qualify under the distributor rules if it applied to the Inland Revenue. In practice, many of these non-distributor funds fall into the category and general description of roll-up funds. That means that all income is accumulated within the fund and that no dividends are paid.

For the UK resident and domiciled investor in a non-distributor fund, all gains made on disposal are fully taxable as income at the investor's top rate of tax. Although gains and income are now subject to the same rate of tax, the non-distributor fund is still at a disadvantage:

- some CGT concessions available to a UK investor are not available to the offshore fund. These include indexation relief to April 1998 and the annual CGT exemption and, in the future, tapering relief;

- the 20% savings rate on most forms of investment income does not apply to offshore income gains.

So, for UK resident taxpayers, to whom this chapter is mainly directed, roll-up funds can be used to shelter accumulated income. That really means reducing their income temporarily until:

- their top rate of tax has reduced. Usually on retirement, but it could also be that a peak in total income has passed;

- they have ceased to be UK residents due to emigration.

It must of course be remembered that gains realised on the sale of shares/units will be taxed as income under CGT rules, but at least that can be spread over a number of tax years.

For non-UK residents the position is quite different and they stand to gain significantly much more, but those gains may be taxed in their country of residence.

Fund charges

The charging structure of offshore bonds and investments generally is complicated. The charges contain a mix of initial charges, annual charges, plan charges, withdrawal charges and other charges – actually assessing the total impact is far from easy. A further complication is that umbrella funds which permit the inclusion of products other than the 'umbrella' manager's products may mean that there are two layers of charges.

As an IFA, I endeavoured to set up an umbrella fund for a client who was shortly to emigrate. The total of all charges, as shown in the 'reason why letter', reached a staggering percentage of the original investment which the client found unacceptable. The product provider, a highly respected insurance company, maintained that in reality the charges would be less because they offset some charges and preferred to show the maximum possible. Nevertheless, both the client and I found the matter unacceptable. Interestingly, the charges reduced dramatically after five years and other product providers now adopt a similar practice.

It seems to be generally accepted that all or most offshore products suffer higher charges. This is in part at least because it costs product providers more to administer and run these funds. I have not found it possible to make a broad assessment of these additional costs. There is some anecdotal evidence that the general level of charges is reducing to come more in line with similar onshore products. The best advice must be to investigate the level of charges most carefully and weigh those up against the charges for similar onshore products. A good IFA could help with that.

Fund performance

Together with risk and charges, fund performance is a major factor both in selecting an investment and monitoring its performance as time passes. As with most collective investment schemes, good fund performance can more than justify even somewhat high charges. As an IFA, I always had difficulty establishing the past performance figures as for offshore funds. It was never as easy or as clear as the onshore equivalents, added to which there was the currency complication. When quotations were obtained from product providers they seemed to contain nice pictures and written descriptions but were always short on past performance.

Many publications state past performance figures in US Dollars and some only cover the previous five years, so it does present a problem.

Do offshore funds perform better than onshore funds?

Clearly, when two similar funds are compared the one that benefits from tax-free growth is likely to perform better. Comparisons are difficult but the best conclusion I have been able to reach is that over longer periods the offshore funds should certainly outperform the onshore ones. Looking first at unit trusts investing in Europe and North America when compared with FSA-recognised offshore funds, the latter seem to outperform the former by 1% pa, but when compared with all UK unit trusts the offshore variety have outperformed them by about 5% pa. I am somewhat at a loss to explain this, except that the strength of sterling may have contributed. The following table sets out the benefits of tax deferral but does so on the basis that charges are identical, which would be unlikely to be the case.

The benefits of tax deferral

The figures below demonstrate the principle that being able to defer an income tax charge on an investment until it is cashed in may provide greater benefits than an investment that is taxed on its returns each year. The investment amount is £50,000 and assumes a growth rate of 6% pa gross.

For an individual liable to tax at 23% throughout the investment period

Investment period in years	Gross value no tax paid	Net value after tax is paid on encashment	Net value after tax is paid yearly – onshore	Difference
0	50,000	50,000	50,000	0
5	66,911	63,021	62,667	354
10	89,542	80,447	78,544	1,903
15	119,827	103,766	98,444	5,322
20	160,356	134,964	123,385	11,589

For an individual liable to tax at 40% throughout the investment period

0	50,000	50,000	50,000	0
5	66,911	60,146	59,671	475
10	89,542	73,725	71,214	2,511
15	119,827	81,896	84,989	6,907
20	160,356	116,213	101,428	14,785

Notes: (1) These figures are hypothetical and are not based on any specific product charging structure. (2) The basic rate of income tax may reduce to 22% in April 2000. If this is implemented then some figures in the first table will change but the comparative advantage of gross roll-up will remain. (3) The incidence of tax can change from time to time; this chart sets out to demonstrate the general principal.

Source: Clerical Medical International.

Offshore banking

Offshore deposit accounts do not enjoy tax-free roll-up so for UK investors tax is payable in the year the interest arises. Such interest should be reported to the Inland Revenue and included on tax returns. There may be a slight benefit in a degree of tax deferral to a limited extent. Interest on onshore accounts is paid net of tax while offshore it is paid gross, which means that the unpaid tax continues to grow and the account can benefit from the delay between the interest being paid and the tax on it being paid. That delay could amount to a year.

Another advantage is that interest rates can be higher offshore. However, many stipulate a higher minimum deposit, typically between £5,000 and £10,000. There may be some people who are uncertain of their total future income and so feel unable to sign the Inland Revenue form R85 to have interest on bank/building society accounts paid gross. For them, offshore banking might provide a useful short-term solution for their tax planning.

There are no depositor protection schemes in place in either Jersey or Guernsey. Instead, those offshore centres rely on closely monitoring the status of banks and other institutions which accept deposits. The matter of depositor protection is under review at the time of writing.

It does seem that, provided readers place funds with a subsidiary of a UK registered bank or building society, then the risk element is virtually nil.

Conclusion

There will certainly be a minority of UK resident investors for whom offshore investments offer tangible benefits and I hope that this chapter has helped readers to whom this might apply. However, there are some real disadvantages and any reader considering such an investment or who has one recommended by their adviser needs to investigate the recommendation carefully and be certain that the benefits exist and that they outweigh the disadvantages.

20 Investments Held in a Trust

Background

It is outside the scope of *The Bad Investment Guide* to consider the background to trusts in depth and to dwell upon all the different types of trusts, the motives which lead to the establishment of trusts or their treatment for taxation. However, some readers will be involved in trusts in one of three ways.

Life tenants

This means that under a will or trust the life tenant is able to enjoy the income from some funds (ie trust assets) during their lifetime. After the death of a life tenant, that income ceases and passes to somebody else. During their lifetime, they do not have the right to any of the capital held in the trust. That means that they cannot have any of the trust's capital for their own use however much they may think that they need or deserve it!

Remaindermen

These people are really the opposite of the life tenants. They no not enjoy the benefit of the income from trust assets during the lifetime of the life tenants, nor can they have access to any of the assets in the trust. Upon the death of a life tenant, the trust is usually wound up and the money (or the assets) are passed over to the remaindermen who will probably have unrestricted use of the financial assets.

There are some discretionary trusts under which the trustees have a discretion to make payments out of the trust's capital or income to certain beneficiaries of a trust. Such payments can be loans or payments, provided such payments are in accordance with the terms of the trust deed and the trustees are all personally satisfied that the payments are right and proper.

Trustees

Some readers will be trustees and as such owe a duty to the trust and in particular to the life tenants, the remaindermen, and also to the person who set up the trust to fulfil the role of trustee in a businesslike and prudent manner. Trustees' principal duties are to safeguard the trust's assets, invest the trust's funds prudently and consistently with the terms of the trust and to manage the trust to maximise the benefits for all the beneficiaries.

In some cases that may be relatively simple. Suppose that somebody left £20,000 in their will to their grandchild aged four, coupled with the condition that the child should not inherit until he/she attained the age of 21. So the trust will run for 21 years. Bearing in mind the effect of inflation over that length of time, funds should be invested for capital growth and one or more good performing growth-orientated unit trusts are probably the answer.

However, if the same £20,000 was bequeathed on the basis that someone else was to enjoy the income until the grandchild attained the age of 25, or the grandchild could only receive the capital after the death of someone else entitled to the income for life (ie a life tenant), then the trustees of that trust have conflicting aims. The life tenant is only interested in maximising income and is not interested in preserving the capital sum of £20,000 and protecting it from the damaging effects of inflation (look at the effects of inflation table in Chapter 3). On the other hand, the young remainderman, aged four, will be less than pleased with his trustees if at the age of 21 he is sent a cheque for about £9,000 in today's money (assuming that inflation over the next 21 years never exceeds 4% pa). If inflation does exceed 4% pa his inheritance will be further eroded. Clearly, the trustees have a problem. This is by no means unusual, it occurs all the time. Every case will be different and the timespans will be different. The age of a life tenant will be relevant here in cases where remaindermen only inherit on death. A life tenant aged 40 with a life expectancy of up to 40 years could mean that the funds will be held in trust for up to 40 years!

The duties of trustees in this respect are quite clear. They must maintain an even hand and balance the conflicting interests of both parties. How that is achieved will depend upon the individual circumstances and likely time horizons. Briefly, some capital should be invested where it can achieve capital growth to protect the long-term interests of the remaindermen and some capital invested to maximise income for the life tenant. The test is that the trustees must be fair to both parties. Those objectives can be met using the full range of investments available to the trustees, subject to any restrictions imposed in the will or in the trust deed. For example, the Trustee

Investments Act 1961 (since amended) imposes limitations on the range of investments which can be held within trusts, unless its application is specifically excluded.

Few trustees possess the skills and knowledge to invest trust moneys, so they have the duty to take appropriate advice from those with the necessary expertise. However, once made there is now a clear duty upon trustees to regularly formally review all the trust's investments to make sure that they all continue to perform as expected, that all are still safe and prudent and that the overall aims of the trust are being met. This is exactly the same attitude and is the prudent financial management which I have been advocating throughout this book. The one difference here is that if readers take no such action themselves then only they, and possibly their families, suffer. Trustees, however, have a clear duty to the trust, to the creator of the trust and to all the beneficiaries to carry out this exercise regularly and carefully and, as mentioned before, to be aware if some investment is failing to perform and consider changing it. The recent court case of *Nestle* v *NatWest Bank* clearly established that trustees must invest money properly and monitor investments regularly.

Implications for readers

Many trustees do not take their duties seriously and I think that there can be no doubt that very many trusts are neglected and certainly not subject to any regular reviews on the lines set out above. In some instances it may not make a huge difference. If a trust's investment is just rented-out farmland there is not much to review as long as the land is let and the rent received.

If a trust's sole asset is one holding of a dated gilt-edged stock again there is not much to review.

On the other hand, if a trust holds a range of investments, particularly if they include individual stocks and shares, then the need for regular reviews and proper management is patently obvious. If the trustees simply take no action in this area and the beneficiaries suffer, they may have a claim against the trustees for breach of trust.

Readers who are life tenants of a trust are owed a duty by the trustees to maximise their income, subject of course to the interests of remaindermen as set out above. If interest rates move either upwards or downwards, trustees should be aware of the effect on the trust income and maybe changes should be made.

For remaindermen, and in the case of the four-year-old grandchild referred to above, the performance of growth-orientated investments should be monitored regularly to ensure that those investments achieve growth and that the performance is acceptable by sensible standards when compared with other similar investments.

Being a trustee is a serious and onerous task. In many instances the day-to-day management of the trust may be delegated to a firm of solicitors or stockbrokers or to a bank's trust department who will attend to the matter in a professional way. Nevertheless, that does not mean that the trustees are absolved from their duties. They are still responsible to all beneficiaries and should make sure that regular reviews are undertaken and all recommendations properly considered and acted upon. If there are no professional advisers involved then the trustees should ask themselves whether the trust is being properly managed. It may be that one or more trustees have sufficient financial skills and knowledge to carry out this task but, if not, then the trust is being neglected and the beneficiaries may suffer.

Readers who are the beneficiaries of trusts are entitled to press the trustees for information and assurances that their interests are being properly looked after. They can insist that trust accounts are audited by an accountant. They cannot control the trustees but they can insist that the trustees act only in accordance with the terms of the trust deed and the general law.

Beneficiaries who are minors can ask the trustees for similar assurances but no more. In the case of very young children their parents can approach the trustees in a similar way. Most sensible trustees would be willing to provide full information for the parents of young children. A major high street bank certainly did that for me when my children inherited money in their early teens. As an IFA with a firm of solicitors, it was our practice to provide whatever information was sought by parents. In the case of trusts generally, the firm carried out regular reviews every six or twelve months and written reports and valuations were provided.

Readers who are involved in trusts in any way will be aware why this chapter is included in *The Bad Investment Guide*, and some may feel that some checking up may be needed!

21 Investing for Children

There are many ways in which children can receive money – gifts from grandparents and other relatives, pocket money and Saturday jobs. In addition, some parents wish to invest money regularly and on a more structured basis. Most of this goes into high street deposit accounts but that may not always be the best option.

Taxation of children

Children from the very earliest age are subject to tax on their income in the same way as adults – age has no bearing on tax liability. In practice most children under working age have little or no income but, for some, income can be significant. A child has a full personal allowance which can be used against any income.

Employment income paid to a child, eg paper-round pay, is fully taxable, although in practice it will probably be less than the personal allowance and therefore not taxed. Employers may ask a child to sign the Inland Revenue form P46 in connection with that employment. Pocket money is fortunately not income and therefore not taxed.

Warning for parents

There are special provisions in place to prevent parents investing their own funds in the names of their children in the hope of receiving the interest/investment income free of tax. The definition of such a transfer is very wide indeed and includes the transfer of any asset. The income arising from such a transfer of assets is fully charged to tax as the income of the parent.

However, there is an exemption in place for modest amounts and where a child's income from funds from its parents is not more than £100 the income is treated as that of the child.

High street deposit accounts

It is a good idea to introduce children to the idea of savings at an early age. For most parents and their children that will mean the use of a high street deposit account. Banks and building societies all have their own rules about precisely at which age children can be permitted to operate their own accounts and many apply the age of 16. Below that age, accounts must be styled in the name of a parent on behalf of the child. In these cases interest is not automatically paid gross but is paid net of savings-rate tax unless the parent signs the Inland Revenue form R85 to enable the interest to be paid gross. Children are permitted to sign form R85 from the age of 16.

So the first and very obvious point to make in this chapter is for parents to ensure that no unnecessary savings-rate tax is paid.

Investments to be made for children without their knowledge

When children are very young and cash gifts are made to them parents have to decide how to invest the money. Obviously if the amounts are relatively small then a high street savings account may be adequate or at least adequate until the balance grows to a level which permits the parents to consider alternatives. Even when children are in their early teens, grandparents and others may prefer that children were not aware of cash gifts at least until they are older and so these comments are equally valid.

Cash gifts received at a very early age can have up to 18 years to grow and, as I trust it is now generally accepted, they will not grow much in a high street savings account and parents should consider alternatives.

Life policies from insurance companies or friendly societies

These can be effected on a parent's life or on the life of the child. They are often designed to mature when the child is 18 or 21. They frequently give children an insurability option so that they can effect a further policy on their own lives at favourable terms. Such a policy can be structured to remain the property of the parent and the maturity proceeds can be used by the parent as an outright gift at 18 or at 21, or used instead for the purchase of a special present such as a car. A friendly society is particularly well suited for children's policies because the amounts are often small and fall within the friendly society limit making the underlying funds tax-free. Children can have their own policies which are often called 'baby bonds'.

They are usually effected and paid for by a parent or guardian on behalf of the child.

National Savings children's bonus bonds

These offer a generous rate of interest which is paid gross and is tax free, the minimum investment being £25, the maximum being £1,000. The interest rate is generally fixed for the first five years. Thereafter, future rates are notified in advance and fixed for a further five years. Anyone may invest for a child who can only hold one such bond so the maximum investment is not overly large. The bond is 'owned' by the child ('the bondholder') until the child reaches 16. At that time they are given control of the bond and can decide to encash it or retain it until maturity at a five-year anniversary above the age of 16. The bond must be repaid when the bondholder reaches 21 or else the interest ceases.

Unit trusts and investment trusts

These make excellent long-term savings vehicles for children. Investments will have to be in the name of a parent or guardian on behalf of the child. Most have a minimum investment of £500 but for those for would like to contribute on a regular basis, regular contributions for as little as £20 per month are accepted by some fund managers. Parents will need to select suitable funds and can refer to the categories set out in previous chapters. Generally, they will opt for long-term capital growth. If sufficient funds are available then parents should consider the use of more than one fund in order to spread risk.

More on taxation

With effect from April 1999 it is no longer possible for non-taxpayers to reclaim tax credits previously attached to dividends on shares and distributions from unit trusts and investment trusts. Tax deducted at source by banks and building societies can be reclaimed in those cases where the R85 form was not provided. I think that that is unlikely to effect investment decisions taken on behalf of children but it is worth mentioning here as a further point in favour of investing in low-yielding, growth-orientated unit trusts rather than higher-yielding ones.

National Savings – useful products

Premium Savings Bonds

These can be bought for children and may appeal to some parents. The minimum investment is £100.

National Savings Certificates

As interest is paid net of tax, these are not generally a particularly good investment for non-taxpayers including children. However, they do have the one particular benefit of simplicity in that interest accrues and no 'management' is required except for an awareness of when the five-year periods have expired and when the funds will probably need to be switched to a later issue.

Index-linked National Savings Certificates

These can sensibly be used for young children's savings. In order to achieve growth over a period of about five years, Index-linked National Savings Certificates can possibly be used in conjunction with unit trusts. Over much longer periods I would expect good unit trusts to do better. It must depend upon ones' own preference for this type of investment.

Conclusion

Children, who are fortunate in being the recipients of significant cash gifts, possibly over some years, can be in a similar position, to a limited extent, to the readers for whom this book is written. Their parents need to consider and to manage these savings prudently because of the long timespans often involved. A glance at the graphs, and other data in the appendices, which set out past investment growth, says it all.

22 Income Tax and Capital Gains Tax Planning

Overview

However good your investment decisions may be, the overall benefits can be seriously eroded by poor tax planning. Readers of the financial press will have seen articles which appear regularly telling us that we all pay unnecessary taxes. That is certainly true. It may be ignorance, lack of time or just inertia. There will always be some who simply prefer to leave matters as they are, even if some additional income tax has to be paid.

The main object of this chapter is to remind readers that this is an area which deserves attention. It is not the task of *The Bad Investment Guide* to try to cover all aspects of personal tax planning – that is well-catered for in a wide range of books. It is, however, appropriate to set out some of the main areas where tax planning and investment planning overlap.

It is worth setting the scene further by reminding readers that it is the generally held view of all financial writers (remember Investment Rule 6!) that it is a mistake to make any investment solely to avoid tax. Instead, investments should be sensible and prudent for each investor and then, if possible, effected in a tax-efficient way.

It is also worth remembering that all recent changes to tax rules have been largely politically motivated in different directions, partially to reduce tax avoidance and (so it is claimed) to simplify matters, although personal taxation is now overly complex. There has been a drive in recent years to reduce and almost eliminate all investments where interest can be paid gross and the opportunities for tax saving have been reduced (ie the abolition of PEPs and TESSAs).

Investments which are tax efficient

All investors, whatever their tax position is, need to be aware of the tax breaks available to them. From time to time these change or are amended, usually in each budget, but the changes are always well covered in the financial press. At the present time the principal opportunities are:

- ISAs.
- TESSAs.
- Contributions to personal pensions schemes.
- Some National Savings products.
- Insurance bonds/capital investment bonds.
- Higher risk investments – VCTs, EISs, EZPTs.

Investments to be held by non-taxpayers

All those who do not pay income tax because they are not in work, or do not pay savings-rate tax because their total income is below the personal allowance, should avoid investing in schemes where the income is paid net, ie tax is deducted at source which can never be reclaimed:

- National Savings Certificates – conventional and index-linked.
- Guaranteed income bonds.
- Higher income bonds (possibly)
- Insurance bonds/capital investments bonds.
- TESSAs (although the extra interest offered may just make TESSAs suitable for non-taxpayers).

Since April 1999, equities have not been so attractive for non-taxpayers as it became no longer possible for them to reclaim the tax credit paid on share dividends. However, since the tax credits themselves were reduced at the same time (down to 10%) it may not matter too much. For some married couples there may be a way round the inability of non-taxpayers to reclaim the tax credit which is explained later.

Investments held by children

The tax implications for investments held by children is covered in Chapter 21.

Investments held by higher-rate taxpayers

Most, but not quite all, investment income will be liable for additional tax.

Interest received from banks, building societies, gilts and other interest-bearing investments will be subject to an additional 20% tax burden. Dividends will be subject to a special tax of 32.5% on the grossed-up dividend but the 10% tax credit can be set off against the tax actually paid. Higher-rate taxpayers really do have to review their investment/tax planning strategies carefully.

With interest rates at a low level, to receive interest and then have to pay 40% away in tax is scarcely a sensible option, except in the case of the usual 'cash reserve' which most investors will maintain. Switching some bank/building society funds into a capital investment bond and then taking the usual 5% annual withdrawals can mean that the nominal yield is largely unaffected and the additional 20% tax is avoided or at least deferred. Such investments are particularly suitable for higher-rate taxpayers.

Alternatives worth considering are:

- Index-linked gilts or Index-linked National Savings Certificates.*
- Low-yielding shares, unit trusts or investment trusts that aim for capital growth.*
- Low coupon gilts – standing well below par.*
- Zero-dividend preference shares (ZDPs) – turn income into almost guaranteed capital growth.
- Some higher-risk investment schemes (eg VCTs mentioned previously).

Some of these alternatives marked * pay out little or no income. Whatever income is paid out will be liable for higher-rate tax but the amount involved may be smaller than the total tax payable if the same funds were placed in average or high-yielding investments.

Basic-rate taxpayers and savings-rate taxpayers

The new 10% tax rate (started on 6 April 1999) is applied to the first £1,500 of taxable income, ie income above the personal allowance of £4,335. It does not apply to investment income from banks or building societies or to capital gains which will still be taxed at 20% or at 40% as appropriate. UK dividend income will be taxed at 10% or 32.5%. This means that non-taxpayers, 10%, and basic-rate taxpayers will have no further tax to pay on their dividends. But, as mentioned above, non-taxpayers can no longer reclaim the tax credits on their dividends. Basic-rate taxpayers do not have to pay any additional tax on investment income/dividends taxed at 10% or bank interest taxed at 20%.

At the same time, the 20% lower-rate band is abolished. So taxable incomes above £1,500 are taxed at 23% and above £28,000 at 40%.

All of this means that there are now more options available to minimise the tax payable on investment income. It may be worth mentioning here that the UK's savings-rate tax of 20% is not unduly high nor is it penal in any way and should not discourage anyone from investing.

As mentioned above, nearly all UK investments have, by law, to make all interest payment net of tax at the savings rate of 20%. This means that the opportunities to receive income gross are very limited indeed and so the main areas of tax planning lie in:

- the use of the full range of tax-efficient investments listed above; and

- making the best use of personal allowances with a spouse (if married), particularly when one reaches the ages of 65 and 75 when more generous personal allowances and married couples allowances (MCAs) are available.

Tax planning using personal allowances

As readers will know, everyone receives a personal allowance (currently £4,335). This increases to £5,720 at the age of 65 and further increases to £5,980 at 75. Personal allowances are available in each year and unused allowances cannot be carried forward or transferred to a spouse.

The MCA is £1,900 increasing to £5,125 and £5,195 when either spouse attains 65 or 75 during a tax year. This is not as generous as it seems since the benefits are not actual 'allowances' against income but are limited to 10% of those figures. So the cash values are £190, £512 and £519 respectively. The age-related personal allowances and the age-related MCAs are both further reduced when an individual reaches a certain level. Currently that level is £16,800 pa.

So a married man/woman with a non-working spouse or one in receipt of a low income may lose the full benefit of the spouse's personal allowance. An obvious first step can be to place any investments in the non-working spouse's sole name so that the income can be set against their tax allowance and possibly be enjoyed tax free. To achieve this the ownership of the underlying asset must be moved into the non-working spouse's name. Joint ownership may have limited benefit – the Inland Revenue allocates income on jointly-held assets on a 50/50 basis.

If either person is a higher-rate taxpayer, the tax saving is doubled. If one person is a higher-rate taxpayer and the other a basic-rate taxpayer then tax is saved by moving the asset into the ownership of the basic-rate taxpayer.

As far as bank/building society interest is concerned, many will aim to keep the income of a non-working spouse below the tax threshold so that it can be paid gross. Higher-rate taxpayers may prefer to let a non-working spouse receive total investment income above the threshold, accept that this must be paid net, and then simply do a claim for repayment every year. That way the personal allowance is fully used and some income taxed at 20% (or 10% if dividend income) instead of 40%.

Tax planning for those over the age of 65

Elderly couples need to take particular care in their tax planning in order to make the best use of their increased allowances and ensure that they do not lose out. They should therefore carefully calculate their total incomes. This is not difficult and just means adding State retirement pensions to occupational pensions, personal pensions plus all investment income grossed up to include all tax deducted at source. That figure should then be compared with the current threshold at which age-related allowances are cut back – currently £16,800. For some incomes above that level, the allowances are reduced by £1 for every £2 of income until the allowances are reduced to the 'normal' levels. It is most important for people in this income area to be aware that incomes above £16,800 are suffering a marginal tax rate of between 30% and 34.5%. This is often referred to by financial journalists as the 'age allowance trap'. If you fall into this marginal tax rate you may not be fully aware of it since the Inland Revenue forms do not make it clear in any returns or assessments other than noting that the 'age allowance has been restricted'.

The first and obvious step to take is to move investments to equalise income and reduce the adverse effect of the 'age allowance trap'. As a second step (or in the case of a single person) to consider using the range of tax-efficient savings to reduce the level of taxable income by placing funds in an ISA or a capital investment bond so that the income does not count towards the level at which allowances are reduced. Once again, the use of a low-risk investment, such as a with-profit bond, can offer a good solution.

As a practising IFA I achieved considerable success in investing for elderly clients both in allocating assets and incomes as seemed best and then in utilising the various tax-efficient schemes to reduce taxable incomes further. The results of course depend upon individual circumstances but very often total income can be increased and tax minimised and the 'age allowance trap' avoided. To achieve the best results requires time, effort and the application of tax planning. This means looking at the effect of taking slices of income out of tax by using ISAs, bonds etc. This is an area where many readers will need the services of an IFA or an accountant but once set up it should just be a matter of carefully reviewing the situation each year after budget changes.

Non-taxpayers (of whatever age and who are married) in receipt of dividends who can no longer reclaim the tax credits have three courses of action open to them:

- accept the position and, as a result, forego the tax previously reclaimed;

- sell the shares and switch the funds into some other investment such as a bank/building society deposit or a corporate bond fund on which the tax can be reclaimed;

- consider transferring the investment to a tax-paying spouse, who will be no worse off, and transfer some other investment without a tax credit into the name of the non-taxpayer.

Although this may seem a bit messy to accomplish there are no costs involved and the tax saved will continue for as long as these tax provisions remain in place.

There are a few other tax allowances available which are included here for the sake of completeness.

Widow's bereavement allowance

Is available to widows in the tax year in which their husbands die and in the following year. It is not available to widowers.

Additional personal allowance

Is available to single people, widows, widowers, those separated or divorced who are responsible for a child living with them who is 16 or over and who is still at school or attending a full-time course at college or university. It is possible to claim for only one child.

Rent-a-room scheme

Income from furnished letting of spare rooms in your home is tax free provided that the annual gross rents do not exceed £4,250. The space let out must be in your only or main home. Where annual gross rents exceed £4,250 you must pay tax on the excess, without any relief for expenses, or under the rules for taxing furnished lettings income.

Charitable donations and Gift Aid

Payments out of your income to charities under deeds of covenant whilst not taxing any tax are a very beneficial to the recipients. Gift Aid is an income tax relief for single cash gifts by individuals to charities. Each gift must be at least £250, net of basic rate tax. There is no maximum annual gift by any one donor.

Income tax planning for those in employment, the self employed and those in receipt of benefits in kind and the tax treatment of company cars and pension planning is all outside the scope of this book.

Capital gains tax

Overview

The provisions of CGT have always been complex to both understand and to implement.

However, the 1998 Budget managed to make matters even worse. For readers, I expect that the principal assets which may be caught by CGT will be quoted stocks and shares, unit trusts and other stock-exchange based investments. The remainder of this section is written primarily with that in mind, although the principles will also apply to other assets such as unquoted shares and property.

The first general point to make here with respect to assets held for many years is that the historical cost of shares and other assets was re-valued as at 31 March 1982. That in itself can be a major factor when considering the possible liability to CGT. The introduction of indexation was a major benefit in reducing the burden of CGT but was cancelled with effect from April 1998 and replaced with 'taper relief'.

However, indexation up to that date remains in place but for gains only, it is no longer possible to index losses or to use indexation to turn small gains into losses. For shares or other assets purchased pre-March 1982 or soon afterwards, indexation relief effectively doubles the original purchase price (see the table of indexation relief in Appendix 3).

Taper relief

Taper relief applies to individuals, trustees and personal representatives. Corporate gains are not tapered but remain subject to indexation. The longer the asset is held by an individual, the lower the CGT rate.

Gains on personal assets

Complete years after 5/4/98	% of gain chargeable	Equivalent tax rates %	
		Higher	Basic
0	100	40	20
1	100	40	20
2	100	40	20
3	95	38	19
4	90	36	18
5	85	34	17
6	80	32	16
7	75	30	15
8	70	28	14
9	65	26	13
10	60	24	12

Taper relief rates depend upon the classification of assets. Personal assets must be held for three years before tapering begins. The gain is then reduced by 5% each year up to the tenth year and after. So, if an asset is held for a qualifying period of ten years or more, 60% of the gain is taxable as is shown above. More favourable rates are available on the disposal of business assets, which are not set out here.

Taper relief is only given on the excess of chargeable gains over allowable capital losses of that tax year and only full years of ownership are taken into account. Costs of acquisition and disposal are fully taken into account (as was previously the case).

A taxpayer's chargeable gains are added together to determine the basic rate of CGT that applies to all of the gains (ie 40% or 20%). Taper relief is then applied to each separate gain in order to determine the taxable gain. The annual exemption is then deducted from the sum of the taxable gains in order to establish the final CGT which has to be paid. Investors with losses need to ensure that they offset those losses against gains which qualify for the least taper relief.

Indexation compared with taper relief

The main difference between indexation and taper relief is that the latter does not start to have any beneficial effect until three full years have elapsed since the asset was acquired. Indexation reduces the gain by a percentage of the capital expenditure, while taper relief reduces the gain by a percentage of the gain itself.

Indexation relief increased the purchase price of an asset by the growth in the RPI so that tax on gains made solely through inflation was avoided. Under taper relief, short-term gains are more highly taxed than long-term gains. This was politically motivated in order to encourage individuals to hold on to assets for at least ten years, after which the burden of CGT is greatly reduced. Whether the taxpayer will benefit more from taper relief or indexation depends upon the relative size of the original expenditure and the gain. Indexation has little effect on chargeable gains where the asset cost is low and the gain is high.

CGT in practice

Readers should not be intimidated by CGT. In many ways indexation relief was fair in that it set out to remove the effects of inflation. One was only faced with paying CGT on real gains and even then only after all costs of acquisition and disposal had been allowed, after setting off losses and after the benefit of the annual exemption. Indeed, it is one tax where it is still possible to plan ahead and reduce the burden very considerably. The main problem often lies with assets held for many years, in being able to prove the purchase price and then being daunted with the calculations. However, I have paid CGT on several occasions and also prepared CGT calculations for clients and found that the Inland Revenue were reasonable where contract notes could not be found and, generally, the problem was never too great. Some readers may have or may still encounter problems with regard to sale of shares in some privatisation issues where there have been later capital reorganisations. The general advice must be to carefully retain all circulars and papers which have a bearing on a shareholding.

It is the widely held view of all financial advisers that whenever possible investors should try to fully utilise their annual CGT exemption limit, currently £7,100. Any part of that allowance not used is lost because it cannot be carried forward to future years.

Husbands and wives each have their own exemption limit and should plan ahead to try to use both exemptions.

Chargeable gains realised in each year, which are in excess of the exemption limit, are chargeable at a person's rate of tax. This is calculated by adding that excess to other taxable income. A basic-rate taxpayer would pay CGT at 23%, but if the gain added other income and took the total into the 40% band then some CGT would effectively be taxed at 40% which is a real disincentive. This is one of the areas where tax planning can have maximum benefit.

If a number of shareholdings increase in value or if one holding increases greatly, as we have seen in the last couple of years in some sectors, then it makes total sense to sell some of the holding(s) in order to:

- reduce investment risk should the share price fall back;
- secure a part of the gain with cash in the bank;
- re-balance an investment portfolio;
- utilise your CGT allowance.

If gains are sufficiently large then the opportunity should be taken to realise losses and reduce the taxable gain. The argument in favour of that course of action is beyond all doubt.

Some readers will have substantial profits arising out of the dramatic increases in share prices in the banking, finance, pharmaceutical, oils, and telecom sectors. It is always tempting to delay any sales and to hold out for more profit on shares which have done very well, particularly when 'buy' recommendations are made at the already high share price. However, the argument remains sound. Gains realised each year (or in most years) must increase net worth considerably and possibly avoid a major CGT problem in the future when the tax regime may be less favourable.

The importance of timing

Timing is always a major factor in CGT planning and the change to taper relief has added a further factor in timing considerations. As mentioned above, taper relief does not begin to apply for three full years after acquisition. When sales occur after that period has elapsed and the timing is out by just one day, in some circumstances investors could lose out by a significant amount. To take an extreme case: if some shares were bought on 1 November 1999 and held until 2 November 2005, four years of taper relief would be available, making 20% of the gain exempt from tax. Had the shares been sold a few days earlier then only 15% of the gain would be exempt. This timing of sales for assets held for over three years will be of most importance for higher-rate taxpayers.

Timing applies in other ways. It is obvious that to decide to sell some shares, on which there is a large profit, in April or May of any one year will just miss the opportunity for selling in the previous financial year.

Similarly, those with larger share portfolios should possibly avoid incurring capital gains early in a tax year as it is not possible to foresee developments later which may have serious CGT implications, in particular, the effect of takeovers where only cash is offered. While this may be rare because most companies offer a loan note alternative to cash (precisely to help shareholders with their CGT planning), it is not always the case. A couple of years ago, Rothmans plc were taken over on very generous terms with a cash-only offer. That cash triggered an unavoidable CGT liability for a client which meant that other, previously realised gains, suddenly became liable to CGT. However, the opportunity was taken by that client to realise all available losses, but nevertheless CGT had to be paid.

Most investors carry out some CGT planning towards the end of each financial year in February and March and then take steps to realise gains and losses. However, the introduction of taper relief makes that a more complicated task.

Further CGT planning considerations

1. As mentioned above, realise losses to reduce gains. If you are particularly attached to a shareholding standing at a loss, it can always be sold to

establish the loss and then bought back into the portfolio. (Remember to wait for at least 30 days to avoid CGT complications.)

2. Partial sales just before and just after 5 April in any year may be a way of disposing a holding without triggering a CGT problem. This can be a good way forward when only one or two holdings are owned.

3. Those faced with substantial CGT liabilities should at least consider rolling some of their gains into investment schemes with significant CGT benefits such as VCTs and EISs which are covered in a previous chapter.

4. If you are unlucky enough to have a shareholding in a company which has gone totally bust and the share price is no longer quoted, remember that it should be possible to set off the whole of the loss against CGT. For that to be possible, the Inland Revenue have to declare that the shares in question have 'little or no value'. That is a formal procedure and until effected the loss cannot be claimed. You will need a stockbroker or other good financial adviser to help with this.

   Even if you have no realised gains at the time, it is worth establishing the loss via your tax return as you do not know what gains may be incurred in the future.

5. For those who are married, additional opportunities exist. If a particular holding is showing a large gain, some of which you want to realise, then transferring some of the shares into a spouse's name could be a way of using their CGT allowance. Care is needed here. If the transfer into a spouse's name took place at the same time as a sale by that spouse, then it could be challenged by the Inland Revenue. It is safer to obtain a new share certificate in their name and delay the sale for a while. If you plan to utilise losses remember that as between husband and wife gains and losses must be in the same name! If you hold a share on which there is a substantial loss which you are reluctant to crystallise by selling, it is not acceptable to transfer them to a spouse or other close relative and claim that the transfer was a sale for CGT purposes. Sales must be made through the stock exchange in the usual way.

6. The use of scrip dividends can cause major CGT complications. The imposition of taper relief makes matters even more complicated as it seems that tapering will need to be applied to every single scrip dividend received. This seems to be a good reason against taking dividends this way except, possibly, in the case of just one or two (perhaps larger) shareholdings. In every instance where scrip dividends are accepted, accurate records must be maintained until the holding is sold.

Conclusion

I do not think that investors should be frightened of CGT, just fully aware of it. I have known some clients and friends simply do nothing for fear of being unable to deal effectively with realised gains. In every single instance that inertia merely added to the problem and I am sure that they ended up worse off. The message on this topic, and its inclusion in *The Bad Investment Guide*, is clear: when you have significant gains or losses – tackle the problem!

23 Do It Yourself or Take Investment Advice?

When it comes to managing your money and investments, decisions are needed all the time. That process requires an interest in the investment scene, time and information. As I have commented before, in my opinion it is a mistake to just do nothing for year after year and hope that it will all work out for the best.

For those readers who are keen to maximise the overall returns on their funds, the decision needs to be made whether to do it yourself or to use an adviser or, possibly, a combination of both.

Many people are good at being their own financial advisers, possibly as a result of doing so for many years and building up a fund of knowledge. They may buy the *Financial Times* plus *Money Management*, *Money Facts* and other publications from time to time, when decisions are called for or when an overall review is needed and they may be confident and satisfied with the successful degree of management achieved.

Others prefer to take advice for a wide variety of reasons. Those faced with making major lump-sum investments for the first time, possibly on receipt of a legacy or on retirement, will find it difficult to handle themselves through a lack of knowledge and so have little alternative but to seek professional advice.

A key question must be: Do advisers add value and do they generate better returns than many people would be likely to achieve on their own? This is difficult to prove. I have only once seen the results of research on this topic. In May 1999 *Money Marketing* published the results of a survey by the independent US research firm Dalbar which compared the returns from directly invested mutual fund portfolios with those held through an adviser. The adviser portfolios came out on top, achieving additional returns of around 1.5% per year over a 12-year period.

'Independent' or 'tied' advice?

The Financial Services Act 1986 introduced a strict distinction between the types of financial advice available to the public.

The first type of advice comes from the representatives of a single insurance company or a bank or building society (generally now known as bancassurers). These representatives are normally called salespeople or tied agents. Sometimes they claim to be 'advisers', but the advice they give is limited to the products their company supplies. If nothing from their range is suitable they are supposed to say so and end the interview. If they are aware that one of their products has a poor track record, or has heavy charges, they are under no obligation to say so.

The second type of advice is known as independent financial advice provided by Independent Financial Advisers (IFAs). The Financial Services Act allows the IFA to advise on all the products and services available and match your needs to the best solution. In fact, IFAs are required by law to recommend the most suitable product for you. The IFA acts as your agent, rather than that of the product provider.

All advisers, both 'tied' and 'independent' now have to pass professional examinations and undergo training and competence requirements. 'Tied' advisers only need to be aware of and advise on details of the products available from their own company. IFAs need to be aware of the technical details of all products available and also the range within each product area, eg with-profit bonds and pension plans.

Tied advisers are not permitted to comment upon the suitability and past performance of any investments that you already hold or are considering acquiring outside their marketing group. IFAs, on the other hand, are able to assess the suitability of all investments held (except possibly stocks and shares) and to advise upon their past performance and to what extent they meet current needs.

When 'protection' policies are needed (eg life cover, permanent health insurance, critical illness cover etc) IFAs are well placed to establish which companies charge the most competitive premiums or provide the best benefits and value for money, as well as establishing which insurers are financially the most stable. They also examine investment returns and, compare charges and levels of service. This is the kind of reassurance that cannot be enjoyed when purchasing financial products via the telephone, a company salesman, or from a newspaper.

This distinction between the types of financial advice available is known as 'polarisation'. One outcome of this provision in the Financial Services Act 1986 is that it has led to a massive reduction in the outlets where independent financial advice is available. For a variety of reasons all the big high street banks and now almost all of the building societies have decided to become 'tied' and, as a result, only offer their own products whenever their customers seek advice. In addition, many high street-based insurance brokers are now 'tied' to just one product provider. Whenever anyone seeks financial advice the adviser is required by law to make their status clear to their new prospective customer both verbally and in writing by handing out a client information letter or a terms of business letter, which will state clearly whether the adviser is independent or tied.

There has been much debate within financial circles, the press and publications such as the Consumers' Association magazine *Which* on the general merits of polarisation and which type of advice is best for the public. Both sides claim to offer the best service. My own preference is wholly in favour of independent advice. Readers will have to form their own views, but the following three examples may help.

1. A male non-smoker aged 40 next birthday could pay between £10.00 per month and £27.80 per month for £100,000 of life assurance over 20 years, depending on which company he chooses.

   (Source: *The Exchange* 27 August 1999.)

2. A woman aged 60 retiring with a pension fund of £10,000 could receive a maximum lifetime income of either £761 pa or £663 pa depending on whether she chooses the best or the worst annuity on offer from insurers.

   (Source: *The Exchange* 27 August 1999.)

3. A man aged 29 in 1974 who started paying £50 into a with-profits endowment policy over 25 years could have received a tax-free lump sum on maturity in 1999 of anything between £108,555 from the highest-paying insurer to £84,418 from the lowest.

   (Source: *Money Management Supplement* April 1999.)

At the time of writing, the whole future of polarisation is under review following the publication of a report by the Office of Fair Trading. The report suggests the introduction of 'multi-ties' for investment products only, such as unit trusts and OEICs, coupled with the retention of tied advice for the more complicated products of life insurance and pension plans. This report has received less than a warm welcome in financial advice circles and the Government's response is awaited.

After many years of vigorously supporting polarisation, some companies which only sell through their own salesmen have had a change of heart. The Vice-President of Sun Life of Canada quoted in *Money Marketing* (10 Sept 1998) said: 'We should be offering the widest choice. No company can produce a product range broad or competitive enough over all markets. If a product is outside our range, we need to enable our customers to access it.'

Some large bancassurers do have an in-house IFA department to which customers may be directed if a product gap is apparent. Those customers should then receive independent financial advice.

Choosing a financial adviser

Since investment decisions will have major long-term consequences for investors, picking an adviser is important. There are no hard and fast rules but before you accept advice find out answers to the following questions.

1. Is the person an IFA or a company representative and are they properly authorised? The Personal Investment Authority (PIA) keeps a register of all authorised advisers.

2. Is the adviser technically competent? The standard qualification is a Financial Planning Certificate (FPC) but that is a fairly basic qualification and further financial qualifications point to advanced technical knowledge. It may be that a sole trader may lack professional qualifications in everything from taxation to life assurance and pensions. Generally, larger firms have wider expertise. A good company representative from a household name institution may be as qualified as an IFA. Prior to the introduction of the Financial Services Act neither IFAs nor company representatives were required to have any formal qualifications at all.

3. What are the back-up arrangements for continuity of service? Will there be annual or more frequent reports and valuations? Will the adviser return at regular intervals to check on any changed financial circumstances?

4. If very specific advice is needed, for example in long-term care, investments held offshore or dealing with large capital gains, does the adviser have sufficient detailed knowledge?

5. Is the adviser authorised to handle your money? The majority are not authorised, often due to the heavy additional costs of professional

indemnity cover. The lack of such authorisation should not be viewed in an adverse light. To be on the safe side, it is best to make out cheques payable to the institution where your money is to be invested. Be wary of any one-man-band operations where you are asked to make cheques payable to the adviser. If in any doubt, check with the PIA that the adviser is authorised to handle clients' funds.

Paying for financial advice

There is now a deeply entrenched view in this country against paying for financial advice in the same way as we pay accountants, solicitors and other professional advisers. The public seems to think that generally speaking financial advice should be free.

Most IFAs receive commission from product providers for the business placed with them. Some employees of an IFA firm may receive a salary plus some commission. Most commission is paid initially in one single amount but sometimes, in the case of regular premiums paid such as a pension plan and some PEPs, there may be a small annual payment made to the advising firm in respect of on-going servicing of that contract.

Company representatives may be paid a salary only or commission only or a combination of the two. Some large direct sales organisations like to claim that their representatives are paid on a salary-only basis, but it is fair to say that there will be a very strong link between a high salary and business generated!

Fees

Instead of paying commission (which comes out of the amount available for investment) some people prefer to pay their IFA a fee, normally based on an hourly rate. Any commission earned by the fee-charging IFA may be rebated back to the customer, either in the form of cash or re-invested in the policy or investment product. This is often referred to as 'enhancing' the product.

Some people believe that fees remove the temptation from IFAs to recommend a particular policy or product which may pay high commission. As a practicing IFA, I was always prepared to work on a fee basis and a list of fee-based IFA firms are included in *Money Management*. However, there were few instances where this service was actually used. In the case of larger lump sum investments it may be worth exploring this option, but generally it seems that the public still prefers the commission system. The latest surveys in the trade press indicate that the majority of IFAs are willing to work on a fee-based system if requested. As far as I am aware, no company representatives are prepared to work on a fee-based system.

Commission sharing

Some investment products, life insurance products and pensions pay relatively high initial commission to advisers (or a similar payment is made to a bancassurer). Many IFAs are now willing to rebate some of that commission back to their clients. That rebate may be either in cash or by enhancing the product. For example, if the usual commission to be earned on an investment bond is 5.25% of the initial sum and £20,000 is to be invested the initial commission could be £1,050. An adviser might feel that was excessive when compared with the amount of time and work involved and so he might offer to rebate one third, ie £350, which could then be added to the initial investment. This was quite common in the area in which I worked. As far as I am aware, company representatives and bancassurers are very reluctant to share or to rebate commission.

The amount of commission earned

Under the present regulatory system, all advisers must disclose the amount of commission to be earned, prior to the customer actually committing themselves and signing the proposal or application form. That disclosure must be clear and straightforward and not misleading and must show the commission in a fixed amount of money. If there is renewal commission or an annual commission payment that must also be made clear. The idea is that the customer must know in advance just how much their adviser may earn and have a chance to challenge it. The rates of commission vary widely. Some investment products pay little or no commission at all, such as National Savings products, some investment trusts and funds placed in building societies. Low rates of commission tend to apply to guaranteed income bonds, some higher income bonds and some investment trusts. If an adviser includes such products in an investment package they may be effectively 'sharing' the commission with their customer. They certainly are not maximising it. Some readers may decide to try to avoid the effect of the payment of commission to an intermediary by directly approaching a product provider. This normally has no effect because the product provider will merely retain the commission that would otherwise be paid to the intermediary or adviser.

Readers of the financial press may have seen offers from some financial institutions to rebate all the initial commission on PEPs back to customers. This could amount to £6,000 at 3% = £180. This was offered on the basis that no advice was offered and the firm simply wanted to secure renewal commission of 5% pa paid indefinitely on the fund value. A similar scheme is now offered for ISAs. More recently, one organisation offered to share up to half the commission on with-profit bonds. Again, they provide excellent product data but do not offer any advice. This will appeal to some readers who feel that they are able to handle and manage their own investments.

Conclusion

Using the services of a financial adviser is similar, in some respects, to using the services of a solicitor or a dentist. You don't have to like them, but it helps! You most certainly do need to have a high degree of trust and confidence. For the best results over the long term it will probably be best to stay with a good adviser who gets to know you and your financial aims. They will be able to form a view of your attitude to investment and risk and may be able to help you plan ahead. Most financial planning involves thinking ahead with regard to the need for life cover and income protection as well as pension planning, lump sum investments and income tax planning. Switching advisers often is unlikely to help with these long-term aims and one aspect of *The Bad Investment Guide* is to offer pointers in this important area.

24 Have I Got the Strategy Right?

Overview

Having almost reached the end of this book I hope that readers will have realised the benefits of at least a basic investment strategy, and that some readers will apply my investment rules and suggestions to their own investments and tax planning.

There will be those who prefer to take no action and those who decide that they have got it just right in every respect, but I expect that many will feel that a thorough review is necessary, in which case it is back to the previous chapter to decide whether to do it yourself or seek some professional help.

Whilst working as an IFA, I always become concerned when told by clients that they had received advice from a relative or friend and that everything was 'well under control'. Usually, the figures told a sad tale of poor results through the application of inadequate skill and knowledge.

There will be many who are reluctant to approach a financial adviser for help and who are understandably concerned at the prospect of becoming unduly committed to him or her. One possible way around this is simply to seek out an adviser who offers the service of a 'financial health check'. That way, one has a chance to assess an adviser and the way in which the financial health check is carried out, coupled with forming a view on the soundness of the conclusions and recommendations. There is never a commitment to take things any further or to implement the recommendations. Financial health checks may be offered at no cost, but sometimes a fee is payable. Whether or not a fee is required will depend upon the policy of the adviser or their firm, or possibly the complexity of the task. It may be that to pay a reasonable fee could be beneficial, certainly if numerous investments are held and if matters have been allowed to drift for many years. In some more complex cases, these investment reviews, if carried out thoroughly, can involve literally hours of work and the production of an adequate written report and a discussion will take further time and expense for an adviser. In such complex cases, my previous firm usually quoted fees in the range of £200 to £400. Sometimes this was accompanied by an offer to reduce the fees payable should some recommendations be implemented and commission earned.

Whether readers take this route or attempt to carry out a review themselves they will need access to *Money Management* or similar publications with tables of current yields and past performance figures. A glance at those tables will show a breathtaking range of past performances and investment returns and yields. Investors are often totally unaware of just how well or how badly some investments have performed. If collective schemes, such as unit trusts, have done very well the fund managers will probably tell you, but they are unlikely to draw your attention to poor performance. Similarly, the Inland Revenue will not tell you if you have not arranged your investments to minimise the tax payable. Remember that a good financial health check should comment upon the past performance of investments, fully explain why any changes should be made and also investigate income tax arrangements.

An investment strategy may simply involve maximising income now, with no thought for the future, coupled with no risk. One step up from that might be to maximise income now but also take on board a small degree of investment risk by including corporate bond funds and/or a high income bond.

A further, and very common strategy, is to decide to sacrifice some income now in the expectation of securing a growing income as the years pass. That can be achieved by moving funds into a with-profit bond, a distribution bond or a UK equity income fund.

Some investors then take this a step further by adding to such investments or (as I often recommended) not withdrawing as income the full distribution available or taking less than the 'usual 5% pa' from a with-profits bond. The result is that the bond value increases and additional income (or a capital sum) will probably be available at some future date.

There will be some readers who have retired on a generous pension or who have adequate income for their needs and invest principally for capital growth. They may be motivated to increase wealth for a wide variety of reasons: to provide for a widow or other dependents, to provide particularly well for old age, or perhaps to help with the education of grandchildren.

Such fortunate people will not be looking for high immediate income but instead be investing for capital growth through a range of investments which pay our little or no income. Alternatively, they may favour lower-risk investments such as with-profit bonds or distribution bonds, and then decide not to take any withdrawals at all. This is a valid investment strategy which can easily be linked with making investments in such areas as UK Growth or International Growth.

Overall investment strategy involves the balancing of income with growth, getting tax planning as favourable as possible and, of course, managing investment risk. Generally, as people get older the less that investment risk appeals (unless one is a hardened investor who enjoys the risks). As the years pass a peron's investment strategy will tend towards investments to reduce risk. It is always important to remember that it is the overall risk that matters. Overall investment risk can, very easily, be reduced by the simple matter of retaining funds in bank/building society accounts and National Savings. The downside, of course, is no real income or capital growth.

The specimen portfolios which follow do not include any funds placed in banks/building societies and I have assumed that a sensible amount will be retained there before any funds are committed to other investments. Those deposits can be viewed as a 'cash reserve' of maybe three months' income or an amount of perhaps £10,000. If overall risk is to be reduced this way as is suggested above, a decision could be taken to retain 25% or 50% of total investment capital.

Investing money is a bit like growing seeds. Unless they are taken out of the packet then planted, watered and looked after they will not grow!

Planning your investments is a bit like planning a holiday. Few turn up at an airport with no holiday booked, no flights booked and no idea where they want to go. Most spend hours thinking about holidays, then making broad plans and then reading brochures and going to see a travel agent. Even after a holiday is booked, many spend considerable time reading up about their holiday destination. Of course, many will think that holiday planning is much more enjoyable but I wonder which deserves the most effort?

Specimen portfolios

I have tried to avoid including specimen portfolios in this book, partly because the range of investment options is large and also because views on investment risk vary widely and the permutations are great. However, it does seem that some examples may be helpful and five are included for people between the ages of 30 and 75, with very brief details included at the top of each. It is simply not possible to include all the personal background information that would be relevant before actually recommending, and then deciding upon, individual investments. Indeed, minor variations in personal circumstances for each age group would alter the recommendations so these specimen portfolios paint a very broad picture.

Some further general points need to be made. In every case, corporate bonds have been included because they best lend themselves for inclusion in an ISA rather than an UK Growth unit trust with a low annual yield of 1.3% (*Money Management*, August 1999).

I have also included distribution bonds and with-profits bonds although, to some degree, they are interchangeable (by now I trust that readers are aware of the differences in that in very favourable stock market conditions distribution bonds will probably do better, but with-profits bonds are safer).

Portfolio 1

Age	30 – 45
Aim	Long-term growth. No income needed now
Risk	Medium risk acceptable

Low risk	10%	Corporate bond fund
	20%	Distribution bond
Medium risk	50%	UK Equity Growth unit trusts, and/or investments trusts
Medium to higher risk	15%	Unit trusts or investment trusts investing in Europe
Higher risk	5%	Unit trusts in Emerging Markets or the Far East
	100%	

Portfolio 2

Age	30 – 45
Aim	Long-term growth. No income needed now
Risk	Lower overall risk required

Low risk	10%–20%	Corporate bonds
	20%–50%	With-profits bond
Medium risk	30%–50%	UK Equity Growth unit trusts or investment trusts
	100%	

Portfolio 3

Age	55 (just retired)	
Aim	Income needed now (pension modest). Requires increasing income plus some capital growth	
Risk	Medium risk acceptable	
Low risk	10%	Corporate bond fund
	10%	Higher income bond
	30%	Distribution bond
Medium risk	35%	UK Equity Income funds
Higher risk	15%	Unit trusts in Technology, Europe and the Far East
	100%	

Portfolio 4

Age	60 (retired)	
Aim	To maximise income but also aim for some income growth (low pension). Not very interested in capital growth	
Risk	Low overall risk required	
Low risk	20%	Corporate bond funds
	15%	Higher income bonds
	25%	Distribution bonds
	25%	With-profit bonds
	15%	UK Equity & Bond unit trust
	100%	

Portfolio 5

Age	75	
Aim	To maximise income. No priority for increasing income and no requirement for capital growth	
Risk	Low overall risk to capital or to income	
Low risk	50%	Corporate bond funds
	20%	Higher Income fund (a low risk one selected)
	10%–20%	National Savings Pensioners Bond
	10%–20%	With-profits bond (maximum withdrawals taken)
	100%	

With regard to all of these portfolios, it is not absolutely necessary to use the full range of products listed in each risk area as all the products listed are broadly suitable within each area. The larger the funds available for investment, then the more likely it is that, for example, more than one corporate bond fund or investment bond would be used. That has to be balanced against having more individual investments than a person can manage.

While index tracker funds have not been specifically included, they could be suitable for those who are attracted to the concept and may be viewed as a way of simplifying the investment process.

Conclusion

Whenever I become worried over the UK stock market and the effect of falls in my own shares, unit trusts and investment trusts, I do three things. First, I get out and look at the 'Effects of Inflation Table'; second, I look at the charts and data in Appendices 1 and 2 which shows the long-term increase in share values over many years; and, third, I look at the income payouts (eg the Schroder Income fund figures included in Chapter 6).

Although that does not entirely dispel immediate concerns it invariably reminds me of the benefits of taking investment risks over the years and also the benefits of having at least some of one's funds where they have a chance to grow.

Appendices

Contents

1 UK Financial History 1945–1998   *165*

2 Record of Past Growth in the UK Stock Market as Demonstrated by Some Collective Investment Schemes   *167*

3 Indexation Table for Capital Gains Tax   *176*

4 Record of Annual Inflation and the Retail Price Index (RPI)   *178*

5 Guide to National Savings   *180*

6 Details of Some Zero Dividend Preference Shares (ZDPs)   *182*

7 Staircase of Investment Risk   *184*

8 Risk Warning Notice   *185*

9 The Costs of Buying and Selling Shares   *187*

10 An Explanation of Price/Earnings Ratio (P/E Ratio)   *191*

11 A Brief Explanation of Derivatives   *193*

Appendix 1

UK Financial History 1945–1998

See overleaf.

UK Financial History 1945-1998

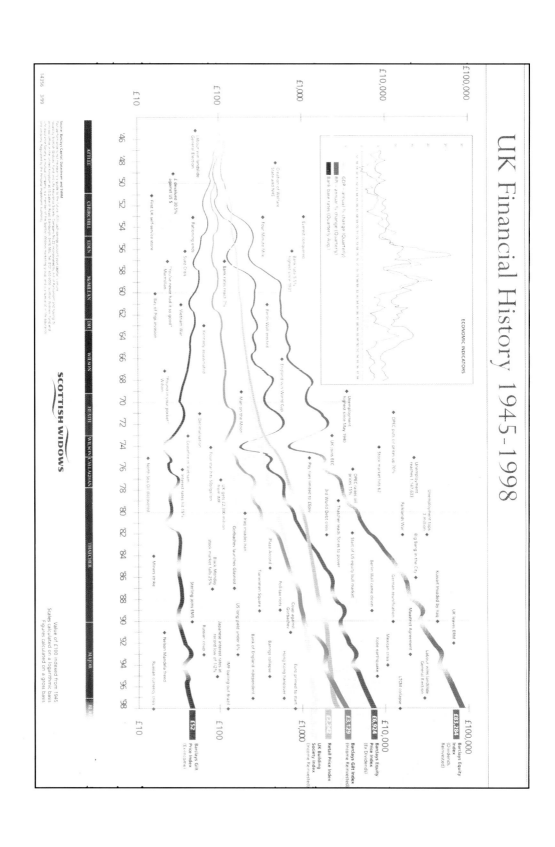

ECONOMIC INDICATORS

GDP - annual % change (Quarterly)
RPI - annual % change (Quarterly)
Bank Base rates (Quarterly Avg.)

£83,284. Barclays Equity Index (Dividends Reinvested)

£6,924. Barclays Equity Price Index (Ex Dividends)

£3,129. Barclays Gilt Index (Income Reinvested)

Retail Price Index

UK Building Society Index (Income Reinvested)

£52. Barclays Gilt Price Index (Ex-Income)

SCOTTISH WIDOWS

ATTLEE · CHURCHILL · EDEN · McMILLAN · D·H · WILSON · HEATH · WILSON · CALLAGHAN · THATCHER · MAJOR · BL

Value of £100 indexed from 1945
Scales calculated on a logarithmic basis
Figures calculated on a gross basis

Source: Barclays Capital, Datastream and SWIM

14356   3/99

Appendix 2

Record of Past Growth in the UK Stock Market as Demonstrated by Some Collective Investment Schemes

There have been numerous occasions in this book where I have referred to the past performance record of growth in stock markets both in the UK and Overseas. In addition, in Chapter 6 I have set out the past annual growth rates of various sectors of unit trusts and investment trusts, coupled with growth rates for some higher-risk sectors. There is reference to the growth of with-profit bonds and of property.

However, in order to provide a comprehensive guide, certain graphs and charts are included in this appendix of actual results achieved by various investment houses over differing timespans.

The products chosen do not have the same investment aims and therefore not the same risk profiles. I have deliberately steered clear of the very best performers in order to paint the broad picture. Figures for capital growth and income growth for the Schroder Income fund are set out at length in Chapter 6.

Included here are:

- Sun Life Distribution Bond – a low-risk distribution bond
- Perpetual Income Fund – an income-orientated unit trust
- M & G Growth Fund – an growth-orientated unit trust

M & G have kindly provided graphs for past performance over both 10 and 20 years. In addition, there are inflation-adjusted graphs for those periods so readers can see the real growth achieved.

As mentioned in the opening pages, details of past performance of individual investment products is included only to help demonstrate the points being made and imply no suggestion or recommendation that readers should invest in those particular products themselves. Remember that asset-

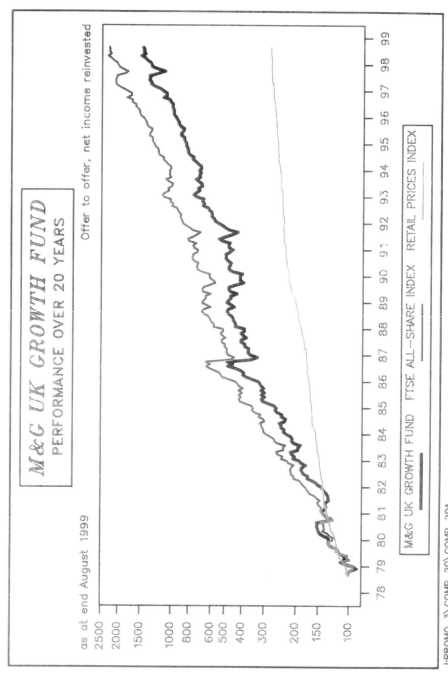

M&G UK GROWTH FUND
PERFORMANCE OVER 20 YEARS

as at end August 1999

Offer to offer, net income reinvested

M&G UK GROWTH FUND   FTSE ALL—SHARE INDEX   RETAIL PRICES INDEX

J:PROMO_3\COMP_20\COMP_20A

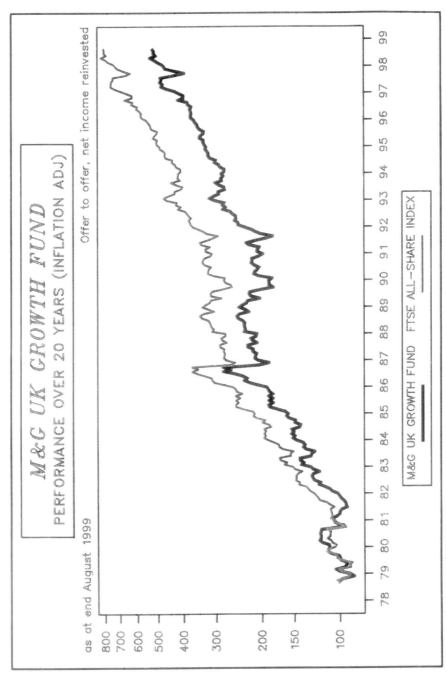

M&G UK GROWTH FUND
PERFORMANCE OVER 20 YEARS (INFLATION ADJ)

as at end August 1999

Offer to offer, net income reinvested

M&G UK GROWTH FUND ——   FTSE ALL–SHARE INDEX ——

J:PROMO_3\COMP_20\COMP_20B

Appendix 5

Guide to National Savings

See opposite.

Source: National Savings and *Moneyfacts*

Summary Chart

Coloured type indicates changes since previous edition.

All interest rates are per annum (pa).

Correct at 8 October 1999

	INDIVIDUAL SAVINGS ACCOUNT	SAVINGS CERTIFICATES FIXED INTEREST	SAVINGS CERTIFICATES INDEX-LINKED	CHILDREN'S BONUS BONDS	FIRST OPTION BONDS	CAPITAL BONDS	PENSIONERS BONDS	INCOME BONDS	INVESTMENT ACCOUNT	ORDINARY ACCOUNT	PREMIUM BONDS
Leaflet	NSA 776/99/02	NSA 760/99/01		DNS 769/97/01	DNS 770/96/02	DNS 398/96/01	NSA 770/96/03	DNS 767/96/02	DNS 761/97/01	DNS 768/97/01	NSA 765/99/03
Interest											
Tax											
Purchase and holding limits											
Who may invest											
Notice for repayment											
Repayment terms											
Other features											
Office address											

NSA 901/99/10
Issued by National Savings, London W14 8SD

Appendix 6

Details of Some Zero Dividend Preference Shares (ZDPs)

A zero dividend preference share is a share that has a predetermined rate of capital growth.

This is a sample of approximately half of all the ZDPs available in July 1999, taken from data supplied by AITC.

Definition of hurdle rate

A hurdle rate is the compound annual rate of growth of the total assets required between now and the wind-up date if there is to be sufficient to repay the shareholders the current share price. This assumes prior charges are deducted at their predetermined redemption values at wind up.

A negative hurdle rate indicates that there are already sufficient assets for that purpose and the larger the negative hurdle rate the more that assets have grown in the past and hence the greater the safety of all classes of capital.

Readers will notice that all split-level investment trusts which appear on this list and which have issued ZDPs, except for one trust have negative hurdle rates. The AITC have told me that since the introduction of ZPDs no share has ever failed to be redeemed in full.

The time to wind up, usually ten years or less, is precisely known. This means that investors can choose a 'zero' to mature when needed within that time frame to meet their personal requirements, such as school fees' planning or retirement planning.

Zero Dividend Preference Shares

31 July 1999

A zero dividend preference share is a share that has a predetermined rate of capital growth

Market Capitalisation (£m)	Share Price (pence)	NAV (Pence)	Company	Years-months to wind-up	Redemption Price (pence)	Redemption Yield	Asset Cover (at wind up)	Hurdle Rate (% pa)
19	61.5	62.3	Aberdeen Dev Cap	6-0	98.28	8.2	1.4	-5.7
98	243.3	237.5	Aberdeen Pref Securities 1	3-8	318.00	7.6	0.7	8.3
7	119.5	114.6	Asset Management	7-3	199.90	7.4	1.6	-6.4
91	103.5	108.8	BFS Income & Growth	6-1	179.00	9.4	1.1	-2.1
41	157.5	158.2	City of Oxford	0-2	160.78	–	–	–
29	121.8	108.3	Dresd RCM Income Growth	6-11	179.68	5.8	1.3	-4.1
14	90.3	87.6	Edinburgh Income	0-10	95.10	–	–	–
18	135.5	124.9	Finsbury Income & Growth	1-8	150.00	6.3	1.3	-16.4
13	270.8	269.3	Finsbury Smaller Cos	0-5	279.00	–	–	–
90	72.3	64.5	Fleming Income & Capital	2-8	85.20	6.6	2.5	-29.9
45	58.8	52.5	Fleming Worldwide Income	5-7	83.35	6.5	1.5	-7.3
36	150.5	151.2	Framlington Dual	0-0	151.19	–	–	–
27	158.8	157.4	Friends Prov Ethical	2-5	192.06	8.2	1.1	-5.3
19	186.0	175.6	Gartmore Brit Income & Gr 2nd ZDP	6-8	306.03	7.7	1.6	-2.9
39	191.8	175.9	Gartmore Brit Income & Gr Zero	3-5	233.00	5.9	2.0	-9.8
11	108.8	99.8	Gartmore High Income	6-8	173.36	7.2	1.6	-6.9
28	260.0	–	Gartmore Scotland	2-0	292.40	6.0	–	–
28	173.8	155.7	Gartmore Shared Equity Jnr ZDP	2-9	212.00	7.5	3.3	-17.1
65	163.5	159.3	Gartmore Shared Equity Snr ZDP	2-9	198.80	7.4	2.4	-27.2
65	52.8	48.8	Gartmore SNT	6-2	82.30	7.5	1.4	-5.1
45	114.3	110.4	Geared Income	4-3	156.46	7.7	2.8	-21.7
46	102.3	102.8	Govett Enhanced Income	4-8	145.70	7.9	1.4	-6.5
28	142.3	135.4	Guinness Flight Extra Inc	3-3	176.20	6.8	1.8	-16.6

Appendix 7

Staircase of Investment Risk

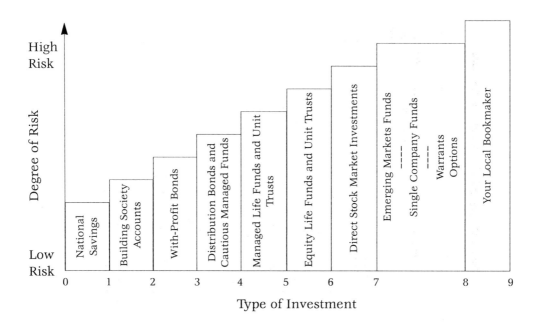

Appendix 8

Risk Warning Notice

- Enterprise Zone Property Unit Trusts (EZPUTs)
- Property Enterprise Trusts (PETs)
- Enterprise Trust (ETs)
- Venture Capital Trusts (VCTs)
- Enterprise Investment Schemes (EISs)

This warning notice draws your attention to the risks associated with investments such as those listed above.

As with property in general, the value of investments can go down as well as up. Many tax shield investments, of which these are prime examples, are subject to an initial price distortion as a result of the tax allowances and other benefits available; it may often be necessary to pay a higher price for such a property or other investment than for similar items not carrying such benefits.

EZPUTs are established to be held as an investment for long periods of time (25 years is typical). Although mechanisms may be available to enable the underlying property to be realised during this period, you may have difficulty in selling your investment before realisation of the underlying property and you should not invest in an EZPUT, PET, VCT or EIS if you may need to sell your investment prematurely.

There is no established market in EZPUTs, PETs, ETs, VCTs or EISs and you may have difficulty in selling or obtaining reliable information about your investments. The tax shield remains in place only if the investments are maintained for the statutory period. In the case of an EIS or VCT this is five years. Accordingly you should carefully consider whether such an investment is appropriate to your circumstances.

I am also aware that the situation has changed considerably since FIMBRA designed this warning in September 1992. I am in full receipt of all the conditions concerning this particular investment and know that, firstly this was primarily for each EZPUT and here the exit conditions were relaxed to seven years in March 1994. Secondly, subsequent budgets and Treasury announcements have resulted in considerable expansion in the area of Enterprise and Venture Trusts such that there are an increasingly number of arrangements to market such investments at the earliest exit dates allowable.

I have received the risk warning notice set out.

Signed......................

Dated......................

Appendix 9

The Costs of Buying and Selling Shares

This covers low-cost share dealing, share-exchange schemes and share dealing on the Internet.

The following are a typical set of commissions charged on the cash sums involved in a purchase or sale of UK equities including preference shares and convertible stocks:

1.65% up to £7,000 consideration

0.7% on the next £8,000 consideration

0.6% on the next £115,000 consideration

Thereafter by negotiation

Minimum commissions:

Up to £100 consideration	£10
Between £100 and £250	£15
Between £250 and £500	£17.50
Between £500 and £1000	£20
Between £1,000 and £1,515	£25
Above £1,515	at least 1.65% of the amount to be invested

Gilts, Loan and Debenture stocks are all charged less:

1% up to £10,000 consideration

0.5% on the next £12,500 consideration

0.125% on the next £230,000 consideration

Low-cost share dealing

Readers will see that to buy or sell smaller holdings of around £2,000 will incur costs of about £30. If someone has several holdings to dispose of the total costs can be significant. In recent years a number of banks, building societies, some stockbrokers and some 'shareshops' have set up 'low-cost share-dealing schemes'. These are invariably carried out on an execution-only basis and always by post, except for some banks or building societies, where they can be conducted over their counters. Most firms operating a low-cost share-dealing service charge 1% on the first £5,000, but subject to a very low minimum of £7.50–£20. In other words, quite a significant saving is possible.

Readers who wish to explore this route should make enquiries at their own bank or building society first. Otherwise, lists of those offering this service appear from time to time in the *Investors Chronicle*, *Which?* and the family finance sections of some newspapers.

Shares held in share-dealing accounts and PEPs

There is move away from the issue of share and unit trust certificates. Furthermore, the various building societies that demutualised during 1997 encouraged their new shareholders to place their shares in PEPs or in share accounts (which means that no certificates are issued). Both of these schemes usually included a low-cost share-dealing option, so the points made above do not apply and readers should enquire if such a cheap share-dealing scheme is available to them.

A further point to note here is that some FTSE 100 companies now offer a low-cost share dealing service for their own shareholders, typically at a cost of 1% with a minimum of £10. Therefore, as an alternative to approaching providers of low-cost share-dealing schemes, contact an individual company registrar whose name, address and telephone number can be found in the latest published accounts or on a dividend voucher.

Share exchange schemes

The privatisation programme of the 1980s left many shareholders with small parcels of shares and subsequent capital re-organisations (such as the division of British Gas) have left holders with a few shares of (sometimes) modest value.

A similar situation can occur on the death of a man (or woman) who enjoyed holding individual shares but where the surviving spouse has no similar interest and finds the situation unwelcome.

Share-exchange schemes were devised some years ago as a way of offering shareholders the chance of exchanging their shares for units in a unit trust, a PEP or a capital investment bond. Conditions of these share swaps vary from company to company. Sometimes there will be a charge, but many firms offering this service absorb all the charges themselves. Some groups stipulate a minimum total value in order to make the transaction worthwhile. Often only specific shares will be acceptable; companies tend to favour FTSE 100 stocks and may refuse to accept shares in small companies, unlisted securities or foreign stocks. This is because some unit trust companies and life offices will only take shares that can be incorporated into their own companies' existing portfolios. If a unit trust company or life office does not want to hold the shares, it may refuse to accept them or pass on the costs of selling to the investor.

Share exchange schemes can be of real benefit to the reluctant investor, who can dispose of small shareholdings at little or no cost and simultaneously move the proceeds into a unit trust or capital investment bond. This spreads the investment risk and enables the choice of a unit trust or life fund that matches current investment aims.

Share dealings over the Internet

This is a recent development and offers an additional low cost method of share dealing. As a practicing IFA I used low-cost share-dealing services and share-exchange schemes but have no practical experience of share dealing over the Internet.

One firm that offers share dealing this way quoted charges as follows:

Up to £3,000 commission	1.5%
On the next £3,500	0.75%

The cost savings will depend very much upon the amount of the transaction. On a purchase or a sale for £3,000 the costs are similar to those charged by a stockbroker, but on a deal for, eg £7,000 a broker would charge about £115. On the Internet this drops to £71 – that reduction, of 40%, will appeal to an active investor.

Orders can be placed over the Internet but have to be followed up by way of normal post. That is the only way share transfer forms and share certificates can be handled. Payment for purchases and payment made in respect of sales have to be effected by cheques.

Dealing over the Internet is not significantly cheaper than the method outlined above. However, the one major benefit available to active investors is to be able to watch share prices carefully and control the price at which they buy or sell. There is usually a 20-minute delay in the execution of an order placed over the Internet. Although the share price may change during that time, it removes much of the uncertainty attached to postal share dealing. Share dealing over the Internet is, I believe, quite safe due to encription and the use of passwords.

Readers may have come across the phrase 'day trading' in connection with on-line share dealing. This refers to very speculative investors who buy and sell shares on-line, sometimes effecting hundreds of deals in a single day. They aim to buy and sell the same shares hoping to make a small 'turn' or profit in movements in the share price. They never intend to hold the shares or indeed to pay for purchases but to close-off their positions at the end of each day and simply take the profits made or accept any losses sustained.

On-line trading is really an option for knowledgeable and experienced investors only – care is needed as it is very easy to lose money this way.

Appendix 10

An Explanation of the Price/Earnings Ratio (P/E Ratio)

The P/E ratio is such an important investment 'tool' that is deserves to be explained at length. Many investors are more interested in the rate of growth of a company's earnings than they are in the actual dividends paid. Such growth has a powerful influence on the market price for the shares both in the short and in the longer term. Indeed, many experienced investors claim that it is the single most important piece of information when considering the purchase of shares.

The P/E ratio was devised in order to be able to calculate what has been earned per share and, as a part of the value of such an exercise, is the comparison of one company's performance with that of another, irrespective of the differing dividend policies. It is called a 'nil basis' of calculating earnings. In other words, it assumes that no dividend is paid on the ordinary shares.

The calculation is as follows:

Assume a company with capital of 2,500,000 ordinary shares makes profits before tax of £500,000. Its shares stand at 250p in the market.

Profits before tax	£500,000
Less corporation tax of (say) 25%	£125,000
	£375,000
Less preference dividend	£15,000
Earned for the ordinary shareholders	£350,000
On the 2,500,000 ordinary shares this is	14p per share

$$P/E\ RATIO = \frac{\text{Market price of the share}}{\text{Earned per share}}$$

$$= \frac{250}{14}$$

$$P/E\ RATIO = 17.85$$

The P/E ratio can be looked at another way. It is a calculation of the number of years that it would take the company to earn for each ordinary shareholder the equivalent of the present market price of each share. This latter definition may help to put the matter into perspective and highlights the vast differences in the value which the stock market places on different shares, irrespective of the current yields.

The main use of P/E ratios is for comparative purposes; this is most useful when weighing up the merits of companies in the same line of business. P/E ratios vary enormously within each sector. At the time of writing the average for all FTSE 100 companies is 26.77. A look at the figures in the financial pages shows P/E ratios in single figures up to about 60.

Generally speaking, shares with P/Es above the average are highly rated by the market for their growth prospects coupled with possible above-average management. Those with low P/E ratios are believed to have less growth potential or are in a higher-risk business or their ability to maintain their profit level is in doubt.

Some general trends can easily be spotted. The P/E ratios of all bank shares tend to be low, reflecting the cyclical nature of bank profits. Most shares of businesses connected to the building industry have lower P/E ratios reflecting the risks and difficulties of that sector of the economy. Shares in all the water companies are on low P/E ratios, probably reflecting difficulty with the Water Regulator and some political risks.

On the other hand, companies in areas of obvious growth such as pharmaceuticals, healthcare and telecommunications are all on above-average P/E ratios. It is most important to understand that any P/E ratio is the market's valuation of that share based upon its last published accounts. If a company on a high P/E ratio of (say) 40 was to double its profits in the current year then the P/E ratio would reduce to 20.

When no P/E ratio is quoted this means that the company did not declare a profit in its last accounts. Readers will notice that in general terms the higher the P/E ratio, the lower the dividend yield. When the two figures are close it is a pointer to a company with higher risk.

Appendix 11

A Brief Explanation of Derivatives

This is a complex area of investment which is unlikely to be of direct interest to readers of this book. However, because derivatives feature in some of the investment products which have been discussed, and because readers will see references to them in the financial press and possibly in 'key features documents', they are worth a brief explanation here. Interestingly, it was the use, or rather the misuse, of derivative trading by Nick Leeson which brought about the dramatic collapse of Baring Brothers.

Derivatives are financial contracts whose value is derived, in part at least, from an underlying asset (often referred to as the 'spot'). Such assets could be bonds, currencies, individual shares or share groups or indices such as the FTSE 100.

In the past 20 years, the international markets in derivatives have grown into a major part of the world financial structure. Banks, securities houses and other intermediaries sell them to fund managers, insurance companies, other banks and intermediaries who can then build them into some investment products they promote. There are broadly two types of derivatives which are traded on exchanges: futures and options.

A future is an agreement to buy or sell shares or other assets at a set future date and at an agreed price. An option gives the purchaser the right to buy or sell shares in a company at a fixed price either on or up to a specific date. Where the right itself can be bought, the option is called a traded option.

In some markets the turnover in derivatives has become very much larger than the turnover of the underlying securities themselves. Derivatives can be used for many purposes: they can add risk to a portfolio but they can also be used to reduce risk. For example, the regulations for equity and bond unit trusts permit the use of derivative-based techniques. These should be used for the purpose of reducing investment risk and cost and also as a means to generate additional income.

A small number of plan managers have set up Dublin-quoted funds which enable them to offer a form of 'guaranteed' PEP. Of the underlying funds, a small proportion are placed in derivatives with the majority being placed on a fixed-term deposit in order to achieve safety and income. It is not possible to establish such packages using UK unit trusts that invested in derivatives. Higher-income bonds discussed in Chapter 13 make extensive use of derivatives.

This brief explanation is not intended to imply any reservations or raise worries over the inclusion of derivatives in the construction of investment products. They have a useful role to play if used sensibly. They can reduce investment risk and need not inherently increase the risks that investors run, no more than a fund manager going into overly risky securities (as evidenced by the debacle over Morgan Grenfell's European unit trusts caused by Peter Young's concealment of unsuitable investments in unquoted foreign shares).

Index

Note: Categories of unit trusts and investment trusts are excluded, as are references to CGT, FTSE 100 Index, investment risk and unit trusts as they are so numerous.

Aberdeen Technology fund, *29*
Additional personal allowance, *141*
Age allowance trap, *140*
AGRs, *27, 34*
AIG Life (UK), *104*
AITC, *69, 73, 182*
Allied Dunbar, *101*
Alternative Investment Market (AIM), *75*
Asset-backed investments, *5, 24, 28, 32*
AUTIF, *48*

Banking offshore, *127*
Best advice, *5*
Bid/offer spread, *34, 41*
Black Monday, *24*
BT plc, *36*
BTR plc, *88*
Business Expansion Scheme, *74, 77*

Capital growth, *25, 27, 48, 115*
Capital Investment Bond (CIB), *38*
Capital protection, *47*
CAT marking, *17*
Charitable donations, *142*
Children, investing for, *132*
Clerical Medical International, *126*
Close Bros Ltd, *101*
Collective investment schemes, *6, 163*
Consumers Association, *151*
Corporate Bond Funds, *16, 52, 67, 114, 157*

Deposit-based investments, *5, 13, 114, 133, 158, 184*
Derivatives, *193*
Direct investment, *1, 30, 35, 82, 116, 163, 184*
Distribution Bonds, *40, 57, 160, 184*
Dividend cover, *84*

Edinburgh US Tracker fund, *29*
EIRIS, *105*

Emerging markets, *39, 48, 68, 184*
Enterprise Investment Scheme, *74, 77, 185*
Equities *see* Direct investment
Escalator bonds, *13*
Ethical investments, *105*
European Monetary Union, *28*
EZPTs, *74, 77, 185*

F & C Enterprise fund, *29*
Fidelity European fund, *29*
Financial advice, *2, 12, 34, 50, 73, 104, 149, 152*
Financial Services Act 1986, *1, 2, 6*
Financial Services Authority, *122*
Financial Times, *149*
Fixed-rate investments, *11, 31*
Friendly societies, *133*
FSAVCs, *105*
Fund performance, *48, 51, 60*

Gearing, *65, 84*
Gilts, *39, 66, 92, 116*
Guaranteed income bonds, *31, 38*
Guaranteed investments, *100*

Halifax plc, *35*
Higher-Income Bonds, *5, 80, 114, 160*
Higher-risk investments, *74*
Hoare Govett Smaller Companies Index, *44*
Hurdle rate, *182*

Income tax, *136*
Index-linked gilts, *38, 96*
Index tracker funds, *52*
Individual Savings Accounts (ISAs), *2, 15, 105, 137, 140*
Inflation, *7, 19, 25, 129, 161, 178*
Internet share dealing, *189*
Investment,
     advice *see* Financial advice

Investment (*contd.*)
    fashion,   *87*
    monitoring,   *81, 90*
    past performance,   *22, 50, 103, 125, 167*
    protection,   *123*
    risk *see* note on previous page
    rules of,   *4*
    trusts,   *62, 134*
    strategy,   *156*
    yields,   *95, 114*
Investor protection,   *123*
Investors Chronicle,   *88, 103*

Key Features Document (KFD),   *42, 59*

Life expectancy,   *8*
Life funds,   *5*
Local authority loans,   *31*
Low-cost share dealing,   *188*

M & G,   *10, 167*
Market capitalisation,   *84*
Maxwell Communications,   *22, 37*
Micropal,   *15, 27, 29, 54, 103, 107*
Money Facts,   *149, 178*
Money Management,   *24, 33, 35, 48, 50, 58,*
    61, 116, 149, 157
MVA,   *61*

National Savings,   *1, 5, 16, 17, 38, 39, 102,*
    134, 135, 137, 138, 130
NAV,   *67, 84*

OEICs,   *21, 24, 41, 52, 62, 121, 151*
Offshore investments,   *120*

P/E ratio,   *191*
Pension planning,   *117*
PEPs,   *1, 15, 19, 28, 32, 136*
Perpetual Income fund,   *10, 167*
Polarisation,   *151*
Policyholders' Protection Act 1975,   *38, 61*
Polly Peck plc,   *22, 26, 37*
Portfolio building,   *85, 158*
Property investments,   *109*

Queens Moat Hotels plc,   *22, 37*

Recovery stocks,   *42*
Rent-a-room scheme,   *142*
Rights issues,   *21*
Risk *see* note on previous page
Rules of investment,   *4*
RPI,   *9, 38, 93, 163, 178*

Sainsbury, J, plc,   *88*
SAYE,   *1*
Schroders,   *10, 23, 26, 33, 161, 167*
Scrip dividends,   *21*
SERPS,   *3*
Share exchange schemes,   *188*
Single country funds,   *40*
Single premium policies,   *38, 56*
Specimen portfolios,   *158*
Splits,   *33, 70*
Stepped interest rate accounts,   *11*
Stock Exchange,   *21, 28, 89*
Sun Life (AXA Sun Life),   *10, 33, 59, 167*
Sun Life of Canada,   *152*
Switching funds,   *34*

Taper relief,   *143*
Technology stocks,   *42*
TESSA,   *1, 5, 12, 15, 17, 120, 136*
Time horizons,   *1, 8, 25*
Trust investments,   *128*
Trustee Investments Act 1961,   *129–130*

UCITS,   *121*
Umbrella funds,   *122*

Venture capital trusts,   *74, 137, 185*
Volatility,   *49, 116*

Warrants and options,   *39, 71, 184*
Widow's bereavement allowance,   *141*
With-profit bonds,   *39, 59, 159, 184*

Yields,   *95, 114*

ZDPs,   *39, 71, 138, 163, 182*